# maran illustrated

Microsoft®

# Excel 2003

**Download** the examples used in this book from www.maran.com/excel2003

*maranGraphics*®

&

THOMSON

COURSE TECHNOLOGY

Professional ■ Trade ■ Reference

# MARAN ILLUSTRATED™ Microsoft® Excel 2003

Distributed in the U.S. and Canada by Thomson Course Technology PTR. For enquiries about Maran Illustrated™ books outside the U.S. and Canada, please contact maranGraphics at international@maran.com

For U.S. orders and customer service, please contact Thomson Course Technology at 1-800-354-9706. For Canadian orders, please contact Thomson Course Technology at 1-800-268-2222 or 416-752-9448.

ISBN: 1-59200-876-3

Library of Congress Catalog Card Number: 2005921494

Printed in the United States of America

05 06 07 08 09 BU 10 9 8 7 6 5 4 3 2

## Trademarks

## Permissions

**Microsoft**
©2003 Microsoft Corporation. All rights reserved.

## Important

## Copies

Educational facilities, companies, and organizations located in the U.S. and Canada that are interested in multiple copies of this book should contact Thomson Course Technology PTR for quantity discount information. Training manuals, CD-ROMs, and portions of this book are also available individually or can be tailored for specific needs.

**maranGraphics®**

maranGraphics Inc.
5755 Coopers Avenue
Mississauga, Ontario
L4Z 1R9
www.maran.com

**THOMSON**
**COURSE TECHNOLOGY**™
Professional ■ Trade ■ Reference

Thomson Course Technology PTR, a division of Thomson Course Technology
25 Thomson Place ■ Boston, MA 02210 ■ http://www.courseptr.com

## maranGraphics is a family-run business.

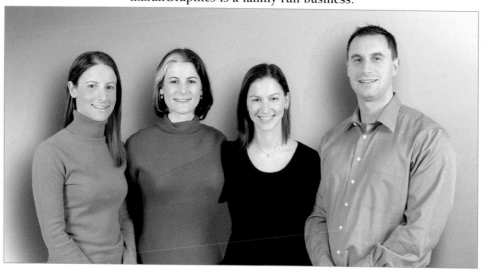

At **maranGraphics**, we believe in producing great computer books—one book at a time.

Each maranGraphics book uses the award-winning communication process that we have been developing over the last 30 years. Using this process, we organize screen shots, text and illustrations in a way that makes it easy for you to learn new concepts and tasks.

We spend hours deciding the best way to perform each task, so you don't have to! Our clear, easy-to-follow screen shots and instructions walk you through each task from beginning to end.

Our detailed illustrations go hand-in-hand with the text to help reinforce the information. Each illustration is a labor of love—some take up to a week to draw!

We want to thank you for purchasing what we feel are the best computer books money can buy. We hope you enjoy using this book as much as we enjoyed creating it!

Sincerely,

*The Maran Family*

We would love to hear from you! Send your comments and feedback about our books to family@maran.com

Please visit us on the Web at:
# www.maran.com

## CREDITS

**Author:**
Ruth Maran

**Excel 2003 Update Directors:**
Raquel Scott
Kelleigh Johnson

**Project Manager:**
Judy Maran

**Editing and Screen Captures:**
Roderick Anatalio
Adam Giles

**Layout Designer:**
Steven Schaerer

**Illustrator & Screen Artist:**
Russ Marini

**Illustrator, Screen Artist &
Assistant Layout Designer:**
Richard Hung

**Indexing, Editing and
Screen Captures:**
Raquel Scott

**Post Production:**
Robert Maran

**President,
Thomson Course Technology:**
David R. West

**Senior Vice President of
Business Development,
Thomson Course Technology:**
Andy Shafran

**Publisher and General Manager,
Thomson Course Technology PTR:**
Stacy L. Hiquet

**Associate Director of Marketing,
Thomson Course Technology PTR:**
Sarah O'Donnell

**National Sales Manager,
Thomson Course Technology PTR:**
Amy Merrill

**Manager of Editorial Services,
Thomson Course Technology PTR:**
Heather Talbot

## ACKNOWLEDGMENTS

Thanks to the dedicated staff of maranGraphics, including
Roderick Anatalio, Adam Giles, Richard Hung,
Kelleigh Johnson, Wanda Lawrie, Jill Maran,
Judy Maran, Robert Maran, Ruth Maran,
Russ Marini, Steven Schaerer, Raquel Scott
and Roxanne Van Damme.

Finally, to Richard Maran who originated the easy-to-use graphic
format of this guide. Thank you for your inspiration and guidance.

# TABLE OF CONTENTS

# Chapter 4

## WORK WITH ROWS AND COLUMNS

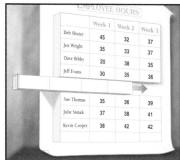

# Chapter 5

## WORK WITH FORMULAS AND FUNCTIONS

# TABLE OF CONTENTS

## Chapter 9

**WORK WITH MULTIPLE WORKSHEETS**

## Chapter 10

**WORK WITH CHARTS**

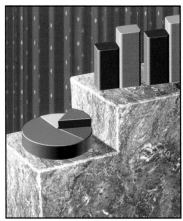

# TABLE OF CONTENTS

## Chapter 11

### WORK WITH OBJECTS

## Chapter 12

### MANAGE DATA IN A LIST

## Chapter 13

### PROTECT YOUR DATA

## Chapter 14 — TIME-SAVING FEATURES

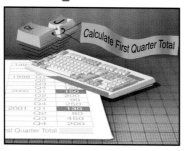

## Chapter 15 — USING SPEECH RECOGNITION

## Chapter 16 — EXCEL AND THE INTERNET

**Excel is a spreadsheet program you can use to organize, analyze and attractively present data such as a budget or sales report.**

Each Excel file, called a workbook, contains several worksheets that you can use to store your data and charts.

## Edit and Format Data

Excel allows you to efficiently enter, edit and format data in a worksheet. You can quickly enter a series of numbers, find and replace data or check data for spelling errors. You can also make data stand out in a worksheet by adding borders or changing the font, color, style or alignment of the data.

## Use Formulas and Functions

Formulas and functions allow you to perform calculations and analyze data in a worksheet. Common calculations include finding the sum, average or total number of values in a list. As you work, Excel checks your formulas for problems and can help you correct common errors in your formulas.

## Print Worksheets

You can produce a paper copy of a worksheet you create. Before printing, you can see on your screen how the worksheet will look when printed. Excel also allows you to adjust the margins or change the size of printed data.

## Create Charts and Objects

Excel helps you create colorful charts from worksheet data to visually display the data. You can also create objects, such as AutoShapes, WordArt and diagrams, to enhance the appearance of a worksheet and illustrate important concepts.

## Manage Data in a List

Excel provides tools that help you manage and analyze a large collection of data, such as a mailing list or product list. You can sort or filter the data in a list.

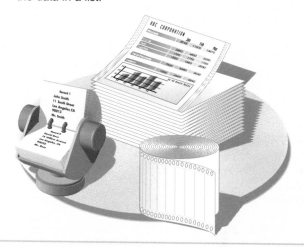

## Use Speech Recognition

Speech recognition allows you to use your voice to enter data into a worksheet. You can also use speech recognition to select commands from menus, toolbars and dialog boxes using your voice.

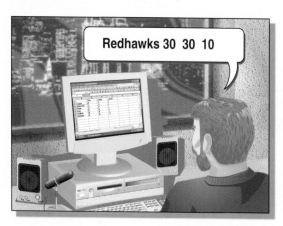

## Excel and the Internet

Excel offers features that allow you to take advantage of the Internet. You can create a hyperlink in a workbook to connect the workbook to a Web page. You can also save a workbook you create as a Web page. This allows you to place the workbook on the Internet for other people to view.

# START EXCEL

When you start Excel, a blank worksheet appears on your screen. You can enter data into this worksheet.

The Getting Started task pane also appears when you start Excel. You can use the task pane to quickly perform common tasks in Excel.

When you finish using Excel, you can exit the program. You should always exit all open programs before turning off your computer.

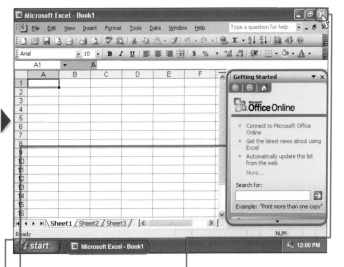

**1** Click **start**.

**2** Click **All Programs** to view a list of the programs on your computer.

*Note: If you are using an earlier version of Windows, click* **Programs** *in step 2.*

**3** Click **Microsoft Office**.

**4** Click **Microsoft Office Excel 2003**.

■ The Microsoft Excel window appears, displaying a blank worksheet.

■ This area displays the Getting Started task pane, which allows you to quickly perform common tasks. For information on using the task pane, see page 16.

■ A button for the Microsoft Excel window appears on the taskbar.

**EXIT EXCEL**

**1** When you finish using Excel, click ✕ to exit Excel and close the Microsoft Excel window.

4

# PARTS OF THE EXCEL WINDOW

**The Excel window displays many items you can use to work with your data.**

**Title Bar**

Shows the name of the displayed workbook.

**Menu Bar**

Provides access to lists of commands available in Excel and displays an area where you can type a question to get help information.

**Standard Toolbar**

Contains buttons you can use to select common commands, such as Save and Print.

**Formatting Toolbar**

Contains buttons you can use to select common formatting commands, such as Bold and Underline.

**Formula Bar**

Displays the cell reference and the contents of the active cell. A cell reference identifies the location of each cell in a worksheet and consists of a column letter followed by a row number, such as **A1**.

**Active Cell**

Displays a thick border. You enter data into the active cell.

**Cell**

The area where a row and column intersect.

**Column**

A vertical line of cells. A letter identifies each column.

**Row**

A horizontal line of cells. A number identifies each row.

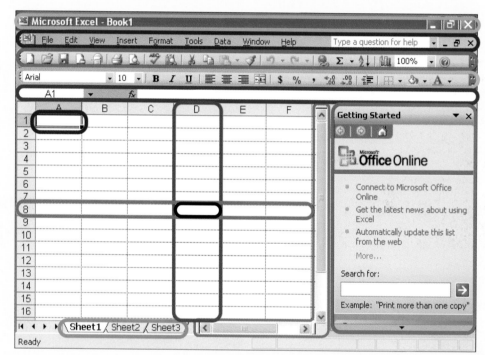

**Worksheet Tabs**

Each Excel file, called a workbook, is divided into several worksheets. Excel displays a tab for each worksheet.

**Scroll Bars**

Allow you to browse through a worksheet.

**Task Pane**

Contains options you can select to perform common tasks, such as creating a new workbook.

# CHANGE THE ACTIVE CELL

You can use the
mouse or keyboard
to make any cell in
your worksheet the
active cell. You
enter data into the
active cell.

You can only make
one cell in your
worksheet active
at a time.

## CHANGE THE ACTIVE CELL

■ The active cell
displays a thick border.

■ The cell reference for
the active cell appears in
this area. A cell reference
identifies the location of
each cell in a worksheet
and consists of a column
letter followed by a row
number (example: **A1**).

**1** Click the cell you
want to make the active
cell.

*Note: You can also press the*
*← , → , ↑ or ↓ key*
*to change the active cell.*

■ The cell reference
for the new active cell
appears in this area.

# SCROLL THROUGH A WORKSHEET

You can scroll through your worksheet to view other areas of the worksheet. This is useful when your worksheet contains a lot of data and your computer screen cannot display all the data at once.

You can use a scroll bar to scroll up and down or left and right. The location of the scroll box on the scroll bar indicates which area of the worksheet you are viewing.

## SCROLL THROUGH A WORKSHEET

**SCROLL UP OR DOWN**

**1** To scroll up or down one row, click ▲ or ▼.

■ To quickly scroll to any row in your worksheet, position the mouse over the scroll box and then drag the scroll box along the scroll bar until the row you want to view appears.

**SCROLL LEFT OR RIGHT**

**1** To scroll left or right one column, click ◄ or ►.

■ To quickly scroll to any column in your worksheet, position the mouse over the scroll box and then drag the scroll box along the scroll bar until the column you want to view appears.

# ENTER DATA

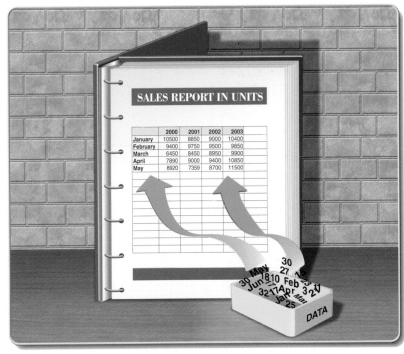

You can enter data, such as text, numbers and dates, into your worksheet quickly and easily.

Excel automatically left aligns text and right aligns numbers and dates you enter in cells.

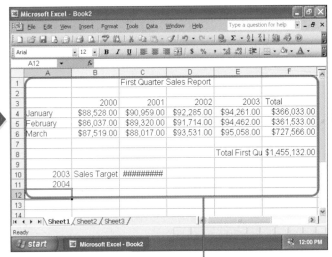

**1** Click the cell where you want to enter data. Then type the data.

■ The data you type appears in the active cell and in the formula bar.

■ If you make a typing mistake while entering data, press the **◆Backspace** key to remove the incorrect data. Then type the correct data.

**2** Press the **Enter** key to enter the data and move down one cell.

*Note: To enter the data and move one cell in any direction, press the **←** , **→** , **↑** or **↓** key.*

**3** Repeat steps **1** and **2** until you finish entering all your data.

*Note: In this book, the size of data was changed to 12 points to make the data easier to read. To change the size of data, see page 117.*

**How can I quickly enter numbers?**

You can use the number keys on the right side of your keyboard to quickly enter numbers into your worksheet. To be able to use these number keys, **NUM** must be displayed at the bottom of your screen. You can press the `Num Lock` key to display **NUM** on your screen.

**Why did Excel change the appearance of a date I entered?**

When you enter a date into your worksheet, Excel may change the format of the date to one of the following formats: 3/14/2003, 14-Mar or 14-Mar-03. To change the format of dates, see page 134.

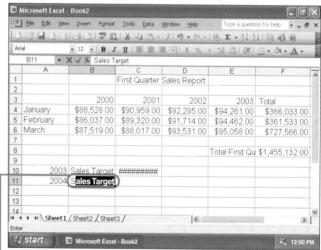

■ If the text is too long to fit in a cell, the text will spill into the neighboring cell. If the neighboring cell contains data, Excel will display as much of the text as the column width will allow.

■ If a number is too large to fit in a cell, Excel will display the number in scientific notation or as number signs (#).

*Note: To change the width of a column to display text or a number, see page 66.*

**AUTOCOMPLETE**

■ If the first few letters you type match the text in another cell in the same column, Excel will complete the text for you.

**1** To enter the text Excel provides, press the `Enter` key.

■ To enter different text, continue typing.

# SELECT CELLS

Before performing many tasks in Excel, you must select the cells you want to work with. Selected cells appear highlighted on your screen. This makes cells you select stand out from the rest of the cells in your worksheet.

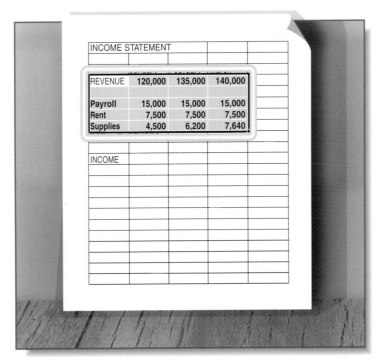

You must select the cells containing data you want to move or copy to another location in your worksheet or change to a different font or size. To move or copy data, see page 42. To change the font or size of data, see pages 116 and 117.

## SELECT CELLS

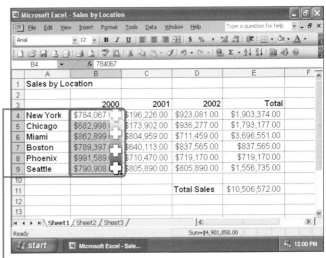

**SELECT A CELL**

**1** Click the cell you want to select.

■ The cell becomes the active cell and displays a thick border.

**SELECT A GROUP OF CELLS**

**1** Position the mouse ⊕ over the first cell you want to select.

**2** Drag the mouse ⊕ until you highlight all the cells you want to select.

■ To select multiple groups of cells, press and hold down the **Ctrl** key as you repeat steps **1** and **2** for each group of cells you want to select.

■ To deselect cells, click any cell.

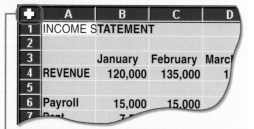

**Tip**

**How do I select all the cells in my worksheet?**

■ To select all the cells in your worksheet, click the box ( ☐ ) at the top left corner of your worksheet, where the row numbers and column letters meet.

**Tip**

**How do i select data in a cell?**

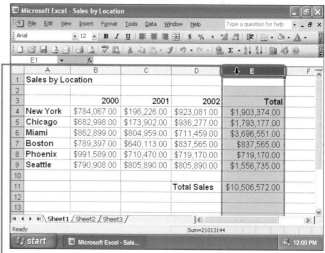

**1** To select data in a cell, double-click the cell that contains the data.

**2** Drag the mouse over the data in the cell until you highlight all the data you want to select.

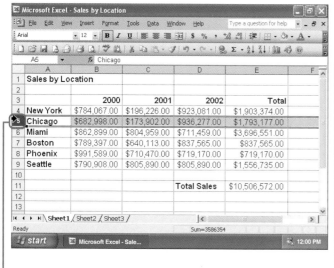

**SELECT A ROW**

**1** Click the number of the row you want to select.

■ To select multiple rows, position the mouse ➡ over the number of the first row you want to select. Then drag the mouse ➡ until you highlight all the rows you want to select.

**SELECT A COLUMN**

**1** Click the letter of the column you want to select.

■ To select multiple columns, position the mouse ⬇ over the letter of the first column you want to select. Then drag the mouse ⬇ until you highlight all the columns you want to select.

# COMPLETE A SERIES

Excel can save you time by completing a text or number series for you. A series is a sequence of data that changes, such as a range of consecutive numbers.

You can complete a series across a row or down a column in a worksheet. Excel completes a text series based on the text you enter in one cell. Excel completes a number series based on the numbers you enter in two cells.

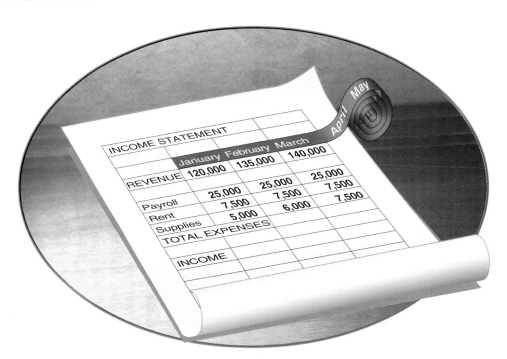

## COMPLETE A TEXT SERIES

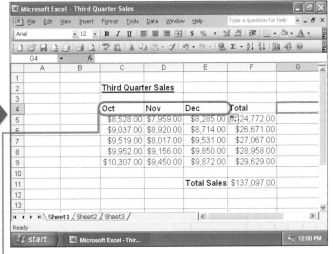

**1** Enter the text you want to start the series.

**2** Click the cell containing the text you entered.

**3** Position the mouse over the bottom right corner of the cell (changes to +).

**4** Drag the mouse + over the cells you want to include in the series.

■ The cells display the text series.

*Note: If Excel cannot determine the text series you want to complete, it will copy the text in the first cell to all the cells you select.*

■ To deselect cells, click any cell.

**Tip**

**Why does the Auto Fill Options button () appear when I complete a series?**

You can use the Auto Fill Options button () to change the way Excel completes a series. For example, you can specify that Excel should not use the formatting from the original cell. Click the Auto Fill Options button to display a list of options and then select the option you want to use. The Auto Fill Options button is available only until you perform another task.

**Tip**

**Can I complete a series that will repeat data in several cells?**

Yes. Perform steps **1** to **4** on page 12, except enter the same text or data into the first two cells in step **1**. Excel will repeat the information in all the cells you select.

---

**COMPLETE A NUMBER SERIES**

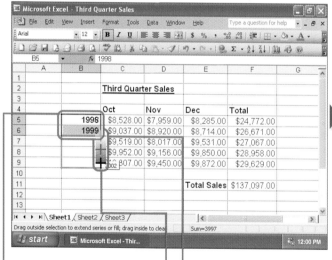

**1** Enter the first two numbers you want to start the series.

**2** Select the cells containing the numbers you entered. To select cells, see page 10.

**3** Position the mouse ⇧ over the bottom right corner of the selected cells (⇧ changes to **+**).

**4** Drag the mouse **+** over the cells you want to include in the series.

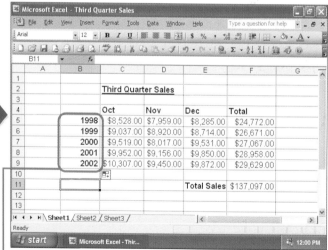

■ The cells display the number series.

■ To deselect cells, click any cell.

# SELECT A COMMAND

You can select a command from a menu or toolbar to perform a task in Excel.

When you first start Excel, the most commonly used commands and buttons appear on each menu and toolbar. As you work, Excel customizes the menus and toolbars to display the commands and buttons you use most often.

## SELECT A COMMAND

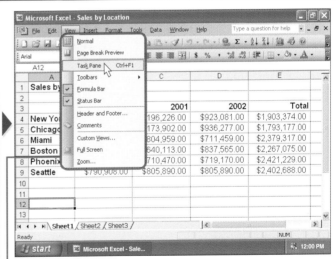

### USING MENUS

**1** Click the name of the menu you want to display.

■ A short version of the menu appears, displaying the most commonly used commands.

**2** To expand the menu and display all the commands, position the mouse ⟲ over ⊗.

■ The expanded menu appears, displaying all the commands.

**3** Click the command you want to use.

*Note: A dimmed command is currently not available.*

■ To close a menu without selecting a command, click outside the menu.

## How can I make a command appear on the short version of a menu?

When you select a command from an expanded menu, the command is automatically added to the short version of the menu. The next time you display the short version of the menu, the command you selected will appear.

**Expanded Menu**

**Short Menu**

## How can I quickly select a command?

You can use a shortcut menu to quickly select a command.

**1** Right-click an item you want to change. A shortcut menu appears, displaying the most frequently used commands for the item.

**2** Click the command you want to use.

■ To close a shortcut menu without selecting a command, click outside the menu.

### USING TOOLBARS

**1** To display the name of a toolbar button, position the mouse ⌖ over the button.

■ After a moment, the name of the button appears in a yellow box. The button name can help you determine the task the button performs.

**2** A toolbar may not be able to display all its buttons. Click ⁞ to display additional buttons for the toolbar.

■ Additional buttons for the toolbar appear.

**3** To use a toolbar button to select a command, click the button.

# USING THE TASK PANE

You can use the task pane to perform common tasks in Excel. The Getting Started task pane appears each time you start Excel.

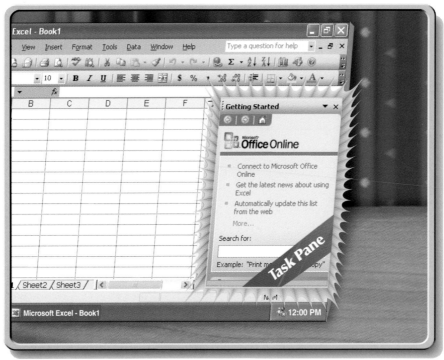

You can display or hide the task pane at any time. When you perform some tasks, such as searching for a workbook, the task pane will automatically appear.

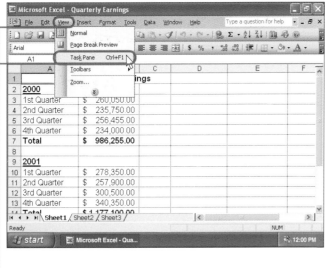

**DISPLAY OR HIDE THE TASK PANE**

**1** Click **View**.

**2** Click **Task Pane**.

*Note: If Task Pane does not appear on the menu, position the mouse ⌖ over the bottom of the menu to display the menu option.*

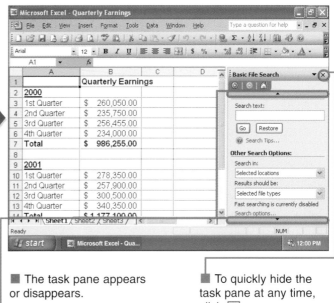

■ The task pane appears or disappears.

■ You can position the mouse ⌖ over ▲ or ▼ to browse through the information in the task pane.

■ To quickly hide the task pane at any time, click ☒.

## Tip

**What are some of the task panes available in Excel?**

### New Workbook

Allows you to open workbooks and create new workbooks. For information on opening a workbook, see page 32.

### Clipboard

Displays each item you have selected to move or copy. For information on moving and copying data, see page 42.

### Search Results

Allows you to search for workbooks on your computer. For information on searching for workbooks, see page 34.

### Clip Art

Allows you to add clip art images to your worksheets. For information on adding clip art images, see page 214.

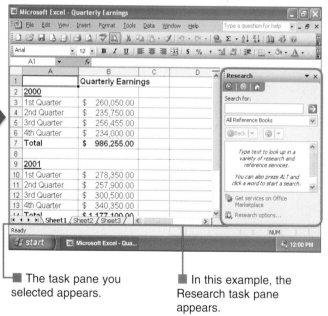

### DISPLAY A DIFFERENT TASK PANE

■ This area shows the name of the displayed task pane.

**1** Click this area to display a list of task panes.

**2** Click the task pane you want to display.

■ The task pane you selected appears.

■ In this example, the Research task pane appears.

# GETTING HELP

If you do not know how to perform a task in Excel, you can search for help information on the task.

Some help information is only available on the Internet. You must be connected to the Internet to access online help information.

**1** Click this area and type the task you want to get help information on. Then press the **Enter** key.

■ The Search Results task pane appears.

■ This area displays a list of related help topics. You can use the scroll bar to browse through the available topics.

**2** Click the help topic of interest.

■ A window appears, displaying information about the help topic you selected.

**3** To display additional information for a word or phrase that appears in color, click the word or phrase.

**Tip**

**What do the icons beside each help topic represent?**

Here are some icons you will see beside help topics.

| | |
|---|---|
| 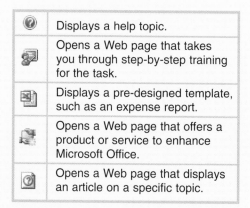 | Displays a help topic. |
| | Opens a Web page that takes you through step-by-step training for the task. |
| | Displays a pre-designed template, such as an expense report. |
| | Opens a Web page that offers a product or service to enhance Microsoft Office. |
| | Opens a Web page that displays an article on a specific topic. |

**Tip**

**How can I get help information when working with a dialog box?**

You can click  in the top right corner of a dialog box. A window will appear, displaying help information for the dialog box.

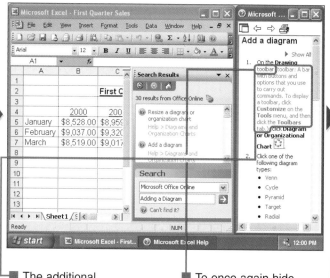

■ The additional information appears.

*Note: Selecting a colored word or phrase will display information such as a definition, tip or list of steps.*

■ To once again hide the information, click the colored word or phrase.

**4** When you finish reviewing the help information, click ✕ to close the window.

■ To display the information for another help topic, click the help topic.

**5** When you are finished getting help, click ✕ to close the Search Results task pane.

## CHAPTER 2

# Save and Open Your Workbooks

*Are you wondering how to save, close or open an Excel workbook? Learn how in this chapter.*

# SAVE A WORKBOOK

You can save your workbook to store it for future use. Saving a workbook allows you to later review and edit the workbook.

## SAVE A WORKBOOK

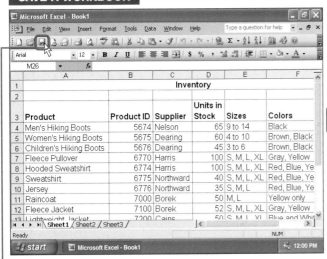

**1** Click 🔲 to save your workbook.

■ The Save As dialog box appears.

*Note: If you previously saved your workbook, the Save As dialog box will not appear since you have already named the workbook.*

**2** Type a name for the workbook.

*Note: A workbook name cannot contain the \* : ? > < | or " characters.*

**Tip**

**What are the commonly used locations
that I can access?**

My Recent Documents

Desktop

My Documents

My Computer

My Network Places

| | | | | |
|---|---|---|---|---|
| Provides access to folders and workbooks you recently worked with. | Allows you to store a workbook on the Windows desktop. | Provides a convenient place to store a workbook. | Allows you to store a workbook on a drive on your computer, such as a floppy or external hard drive. | Allows you to store a workbook on your network. |

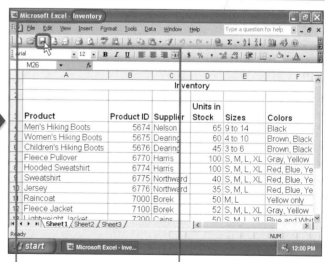

■ This area shows the location where Excel will store your workbook. You can click this area to change the location.

■ This area allows you to access commonly used locations. You can click a location to save your workbook in the location.

**3** Click **Save** to save your workbook.

■ Excel saves your workbook and displays the name of the workbook at the top of your screen.

SAVE CHANGES

**You should regularly save changes you make to a workbook to avoid losing your work.**

**1** Click 🔡 to save the changes you made to your workbook.

# CREATE A NEW WORKBOOK

You can easily create a new workbook to store new data, such as a budget or sales report.

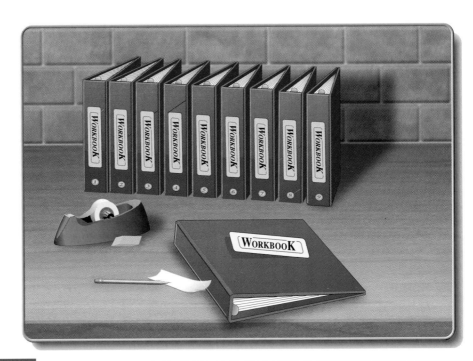

When you create a new workbook, Excel displays a blank worksheet on your screen. You do not have to close the workbook currently displayed on your screen before creating a new workbook.

## CREATE A NEW WORKBOOK

■1 Click to create a new workbook.

*Note: If is not displayed, click on the Standard toolbar to display the button.*

■ A new workbook appears. The previous workbook is now hidden behind the new workbook.

■ Excel gives the new workbook a temporary name, such as Book2, until you save the workbook. To save a workbook, see page 22.

■ A button for the new workbook appears on the taskbar.

# SWITCH BETWEEN WORKBOOKS

You can have several
workbooks open at
once. Excel allows you
to easily switch from
one open workbook
to another.

## SWITCH BETWEEN WORKBOOKS

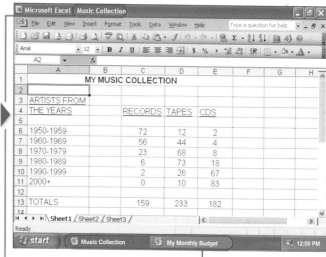

■1 Click **Window** to
display a list of all the
workbooks you have
open.

■2 Click the name of
the workbook you
want to switch to.

■ The workbook
appears.

■ This area shows the
name of the displayed
workbook.

■ The taskbar
displays a button for
each open workbook.
You can also click the
buttons on the taskbar
to switch between the
open workbooks.

# VIEW ALL OPEN WORKBOOKS

If you have several workbooks open, some of them may be hidden from view. You can display the contents of all your open workbooks at once.

## VIEW ALL OPEN WORKBOOKS

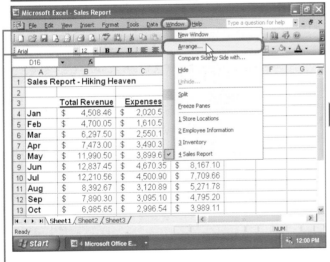

**1** Click **Window**.

**2** Click **Arrange**.

*Note: If Arrange does not appear on the menu, position the mouse ⇧ over the bottom of the menu to display the menu option.*

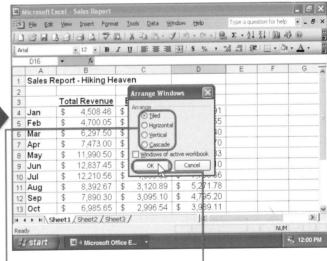

■ The Arrange Windows dialog box appears.

**3** Click an option to select the way you want to arrange your open workbooks (○ changes to ◉).

**4** Click **OK** to arrange your workbooks.

**Tip** How can I arrange open workbooks on my screen?

**Tiled**

The workbooks appear as tiled squares, allowing you to clearly view the contents of each workbook.

**Horizontal**

The workbooks appear one above the other.

**Vertical**

The workbooks appear side by side.

**Cascade**

The workbooks overlap each other, allowing you to clearly view the title bar of each workbook.

■ Your workbooks appear neatly arranged.

■ You can work with only one workbook at a time. The current workbook displays a dark title bar.

**5** To make another workbook current, click anywhere in the workbook.

■ To make the current workbook fill your screen, click ▣.

# COMPARE WORKBOOKS

You can display two workbooks on your screen at once. Excel displays one workbook above the other so you can easily compare data in corresponding rows. Comparing workbooks is useful if you want to compare an edited workbook to the original version of the workbook.

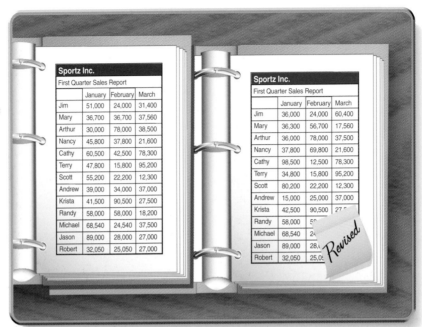

When you scroll through one workbook, Excel automatically scrolls through the other workbook for you, so you can compare the contents of the two workbooks.

## COMPARE WORKBOOKS

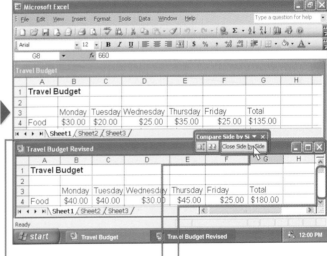

**1** Open the two workbooks you want to compare.

*Note: To open a workbook, see page 32.*

**2** Click **Window** in the current workbook.

**3** Click **Compare Side by Side with** to compare the current workbook with the other open workbook.

■ Excel displays the workbooks on your screen. One workbook appears above the other workbook.

■ The Compare Side by Side toolbar also appears.

**4** To scroll through the workbooks, drag the scroll box up or down in one workbook. Excel automatically scrolls the other workbook for you.

**5** When you finish comparing the workbooks on your screen, click **Close Side by Side**.

# CLOSE A WORKBOOK

When you finish working with a workbook, you can close the workbook to remove it from your screen.

When you close a workbook, you do not exit the Excel program. You can continue to work with other workbooks.

## CLOSE A WORKBOOK

■ Before closing a workbook, you should save any changes you made to the workbook. To save a workbook, see page 22.

**1** Click **File**.

**2** Click **Close** to close the workbook.

■ The workbook disappears from your screen.

■ If you had more than one workbook open, the second last workbook you worked with appears on your screen.

**QUICKLY CLOSE A WORKBOOK**

■ To quickly close a workbook, click ⊠.

# SAVE WORKBOOKS IN A WORKSPACE FILE

You can save workbooks in a workspace file to have Excel remember the size and location of each workbook on your screen. You can later open the workspace file to open all the workbooks at once.

Before saving workbooks in a workspace file, save each workbook. To save a workbook, see page 22.

## SAVE WORKBOOKS IN A WORKSPACE FILE

**1** Display and arrange the workbooks you want to include in the workspace file. To arrange open workbooks, see page 26.

**2** Click **File**.

**3** Click **Save Workspace**.

*Note: If Save Workspace does not appear on the menu, position the mouse ⬡ over the bottom of the menu to display the menu option.*

■ The Save Workspace dialog box appears.

**4** Type a name for the workspace file.

■ This area shows the location where Excel will store your workspace file. You can click this area to change the location.

**5** Click **Save** to save your workspace file.

■ You can later open your workspace file as you would open any workbook. To open a workbook, see page 32.

30

You can save a
workbook with
a different name.
This is useful
if you want to
create a copy
of the workbook.

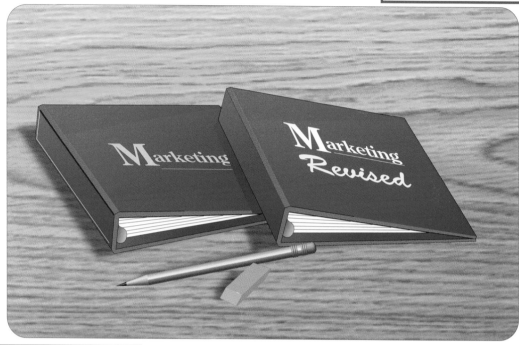

### SAVE A WORKBOOK WITH A NEW NAME

**1** Click **File**.

**2** Click **Save As**.

■ The Save As dialog
box appears.

**3** Type a new name for
the workbook.

■ This area shows the
location where Excel
will store your workbook.
You can click this area
to change the location.

**4** Click **Save** to save
your workbook with the
new name.

■ Excel saves a copy
of your workbook with
the new name.

# OPEN A WORKBOOK

You can open a saved workbook to view the workbook on your screen. Opening a workbook allows you to review and make changes to the workbook.

## OPEN A WORKBOOK

**1** Click 📂 to open a workbook.

■ The Open dialog box appears.

■ This area shows the location of the displayed workbooks. You can click this area to change the location.

■ This area allows you to access workbooks in commonly used locations. You can click a location to display the workbooks stored in the location.

*Note: For information on the commonly used locations, see the top of page 23.*

**Tip**

**How can I quickly open a workbook I recently worked with?**

Excel remembers the names of the last four workbooks you worked with. You can use the Getting Started task pane or the File menu to quickly open one of these workbooks.

*Note: The Getting Started task pane appears each time you start Excel. To display the Getting Started task pane, see page 16.*

**Use the Task Pane**

**1** Click the name of the workbook you want to open.

*Note: If the name of the workbook is not displayed, position the mouse over the bottom of the task pane to display the name.*

**Use the File Menu**

**1** Click **File**.

**2** Click the name of the workbook you want to open.

*Note: If the name of the workbook you want is not displayed, position the mouse over the bottom of the menu to display the name.*

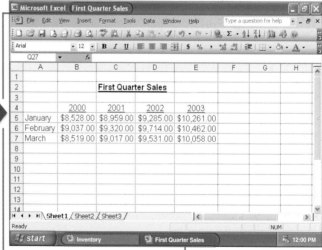

**2** Click the name of the workbook you want to open.

**3** Click **Open** to open the workbook.

■ The workbook opens and appears on your screen. You can now review and make changes to the workbook.

■ This area displays the name of the open workbook.

■ If you already had a workbook open, the new workbook appears in a new Microsoft Excel window. You can click the buttons on the taskbar to switch between the open workbooks.

# SEARCH FOR A WORKBOOK

If you cannot remember the name or location of a workbook you want to work with, you can search for the workbook.

## SEARCH FOR A WORKBOOK

**1** Click **File**.

**2** Click **File Search** to search for a workbook.

■ The Basic File Search task pane appears.

**3** Click this area and type one or more words you want to search for.

*Note: If this area already contains text, drag the mouse I over the existing text before performing step 3.*

**4** Click ☑ in this area to select the locations you want to search.

■ A check mark (✔) appears beside each location that Excel will search.

*Note: By default, Excel will search all the drives and folders on your computer.*

**5** You can click the box beside a location to add (☑) or remove (☐) a check mark.

**6** Click outside the list of locations to close the list.

**Tip**

**How will Excel use the words I specify to search for workbooks?**

Excel will search the contents of workbooks and the file names of workbooks for the words you specify. When searching the contents of workbooks, Excel will search for various forms of the words. For example, searching for "run" will find "run," "running" and "ran."

Search for:
run

Finds:
• run
• running
• ran

 **Tip**

**When selecting the locations and types of files I want to search for, how can I display more items?**

Each item that displays a plus sign (⊞) contains hidden items. To display the hidden items, click the plus sign (⊞) beside the item (⊞ changes to ⊟). To once again hide the items, click the minus sign (⊟) beside the item.

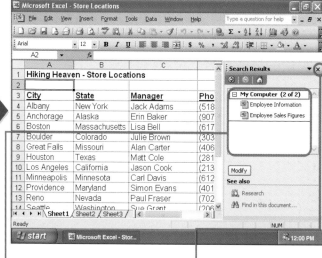

**7** Click ▼ in this area to specify the types of files you want to search for.

■ A check mark (✔) appears beside each type of file that Excel will search for.

**8** You can click the box beside a file type to add (✔) or remove (☐) a check mark.

**9** Click outside the list of file types to close the list.

**10** Click **Go** to start the search.

■ This area lists the workbooks that contain the word(s) you specified.

■ To open a workbook in the list, click the workbook.

■ To close the task pane at any time, click ✕.

## CHAPTER 3

# Edit Your Worksheets

*Do you want to edit the data in your worksheets or check your worksheets for spelling errors? This chapter teaches you how.*

# EDIT DATA

You can edit data in your worksheet to correct a mistake or update data.

## EDIT DATA

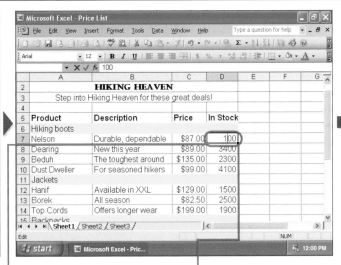

**1** Double-click the cell containing the data you want to edit.

■ A flashing insertion point appears in the cell.

**2** Press the ← or → key to move the insertion point to where you want to remove or add characters.

**3** To remove the character to the left of the insertion point, press the ◆Backspace key.

■ To remove the character to the right of the insertion point, press the Delete key.

**Tip**

### Can I edit data in the formula bar?

**1** To edit data in the formula bar, click the cell containing the data you want to edit.

■ The formula bar displays the data.

**2** Click in the formula bar and then perform steps **2** to **5** below to edit the data.

**Tip**

### Can I edit data using only my keyboard?

If you have trouble double-clicking or prefer to use your keyboard, you can use only your keyboard to edit data. Press the ←, →, ↑ or ↓ key to select the cell you want to make the active cell and then press the F2 key to edit the data in the active cell. The insertion point appears at the end of the data in the cell.

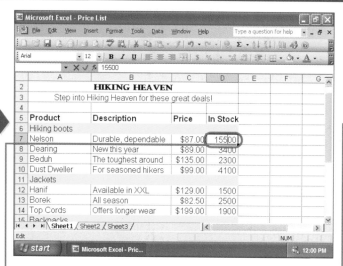

**4** To add data where the insertion point flashes on your screen, type the data.

**5** When you finish making changes to the data, press the Enter key.

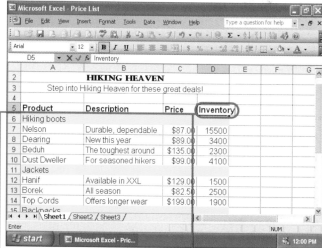

**REPLACE ALL DATA IN A CELL**

**1** Click the cell containing the data you want to replace with new data.

**2** Type the new data and then press the Enter key.

# DELETE DATA

You can remove data you no longer need from cells in your worksheet. You can delete data from a single cell or from several cells at once.

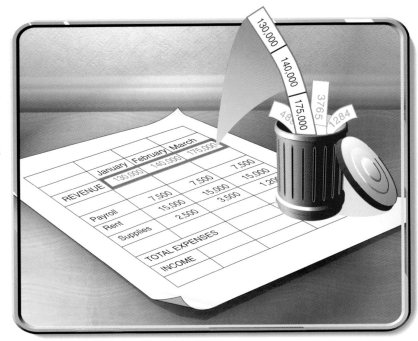

When you delete the data in a cell, Excel does not remove the formatting you applied to the cell, such as a new font or color. Any new data you enter into the cell will display the same formatting as the data you deleted. To clear the formatting from cells, see the top of page 137.

To clear the formatting from cells, see the top of page 137.

## DELETE DATA

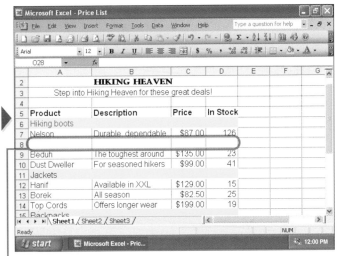

**1** Select the cells containing the data you want to delete. To select cells, see page 10.

**2** Press the Delete key.

■ The data in the cells you selected disappears.

■ To deselect cells, click any cell.

40

# UNDO CHANGES

Excel remembers the last changes you made to your worksheet. If you regret these changes, you can cancel them by using the Undo feature.

The Undo feature can cancel your last editing and formatting changes. If you do not like the results of canceling an editing or formatting change, you can easily reverse the results.

## UNDO CHANGES

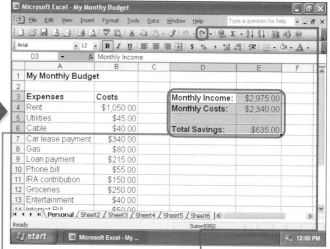

**1** Click ⤺ to undo the last change you made to your worksheet.

*Note: If ⤺ is not displayed, click ⁝ on the Standard toolbar to display the button.*

■ Excel cancels the last change you made to your worksheet.

■ You can repeat step **1** to cancel previous changes you made.

■ To reverse the results of using the Undo feature, click ⤻.

*Note: If ⤻ is not displayed, click ⁝ on the Standard toolbar to display the button.*

# MOVE OR COPY DATA

**You can move or copy data to a new location in your worksheet.**

Moving data allows you to reorganize data in your worksheet. When you move data, the data disappears from its original location.

Copying data allows you to repeat data in your worksheet without having to retype the data. When you copy data, the data appears in both the original and new locations.

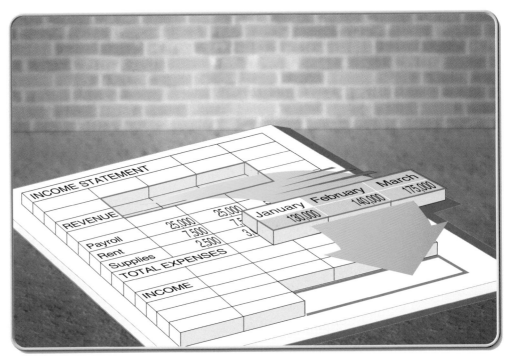

## MOVE OR COPY DATA

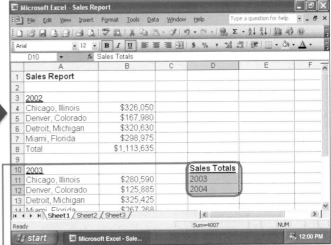

**USING DRAG AND DROP**

**1** Select the cells containing the data you want to move. To select cells, see page 10.

**2** Position the mouse ⊡ over a border of the selected cells (⊡ changes to ⊹).

**3** To move the data, drag the mouse ⊳ to where you want to place the data.

*Note: A gray box indicates where the data will appear.*

■ The data moves to the new location.

■ To copy data, perform steps **1** to **3**, except press and hold down the **Ctrl** key as you perform step **3**.

**Tip**

### How can I use the Clipboard task pane to move or copy data?

The Clipboard task pane displays the last 24 items you have selected to move or copy using the toolbar buttons. To display the Clipboard task pane, see page 16. To place a clipboard item into your worksheet, click the cell where you want to place the item and then click the item in the task pane.

**Tip**

### Why does the Paste Options button (📋) appear when I copy data?

You can use the Paste Options button (📋) to change the way Excel copies data when you use the Copy button (🖹). For example, you can specify that you want to copy only the formatting of the original cells to the new location. Click the Paste Options button to display a list of options and then select the option you want to use. The Paste Options button is available only until you perform another task.

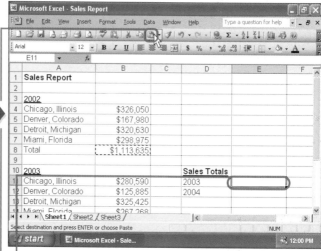

**USING THE TOOLBAR BUTTONS**

**1** Select the cells containing the data you want to move or copy. To select cells, see page 10.

**2** Click one of the following buttons.

✂ Move data

📋 Copy data

**3** Click the cell where you want to place the data. This cell will become the top left cell of the new location.

**4** Click 🖹 to place the data in the new location.

■ The data appears in the new location.

*Note: A moving, dotted border may appear around the cells you selected to move or copy. To remove the border, press the* `Esc` *key.*

# CHECK SPELLING

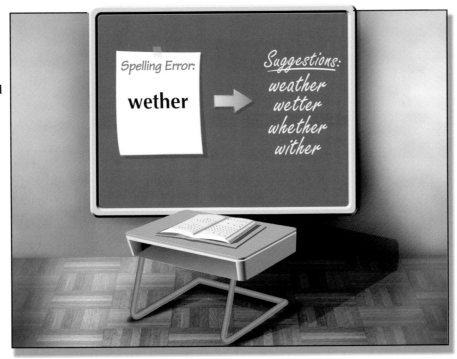

You can find and correct all the spelling errors in your worksheet.

Excel compares every word in your worksheet to words in its dictionary. If a word in your worksheet does not exist in the dictionary, the word is considered misspelled.

CHECK SPELLING

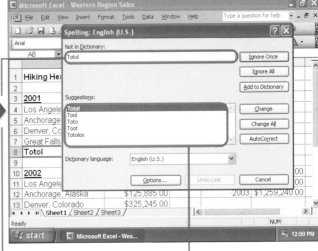

**1** Click cell **A1** to start the spell check at the beginning of your worksheet.

**2** Click [icon] to start the spell check.

■ The Spelling dialog box appears if Excel finds a misspelled word.

■ This area displays the misspelled word.

■ This area displays suggestions for correcting the word.

**Tip**

**What parts of a worksheet does Excel check for spelling errors?**

In addition to text in cells, Excel spell checks text in items such as comments, charts, AutoShapes, text boxes, diagrams and headers and footers.

**Tip**

**Can Excel automatically correct my typing mistakes?**

Yes. Excel automatically corrects common spelling errors as you type. Here are a few examples.

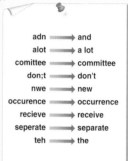

| adn | → and |
|---|---|
| alot | → a lot |
| comittee | → committee |
| don;t | → don't |
| nwe | → new |
| occurence | → occurrence |
| recieve | → receive |
| seperate | → separate |
| teh | → the |

To view a complete list of the spelling errors that Excel will automatically correct, perform the steps on page 46.

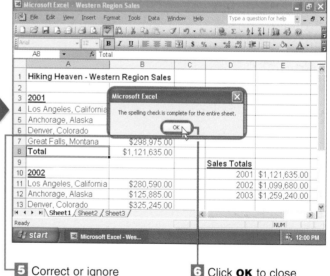

**3** To select one of the suggestions, click the suggestion.

**4** Click **Change** to correct the word in your worksheet.

■ To skip the word and continue checking your worksheet, click **Ignore Once**.

*Note: To skip the word and all occurrences of the word in your worksheet, click Ignore All.*

**5** Correct or ignore misspelled words until this dialog box appears, telling you the spell check is complete.

**6** Click **OK** to close the dialog box.

# USING AUTOCORRECT

Excel automatically corrects hundreds of common typing and spelling errors as you type. You can create an AutoCorrect entry to add your own words and phrases to the list of errors that Excel corrects.

| | | |
|---|---|---|
| (c) | ⟹ | © |
| (tm) | ⟹ | TM |
| accordingto | ⟹ | according to |
| ahve | ⟹ | have |
| can;t | ⟹ | can't |
| chnage | ⟹ | change |
| may of been | ⟹ | may have been |
| recieve | ⟹ | receive |
| seperate | ⟹ | separate |
| teh | ⟹ | the |

## USING AUTOCORRECT

**1** Click **Tools**.

**2** Click **AutoCorrect Options**.

*Note: If AutoCorrect Options does not appear on the menu, position the mouse ⟍ over the bottom of the menu to display the menu option.*

■ The AutoCorrect dialog box appears.

■ This area displays the list of AutoCorrect entries included with Excel.

**Tip**

### What other types of errors does Excel automatically correct?

When you type two consecutive uppercase letters, Excel automatically converts the second letter to lowercase. When you type a lowercase letter as the first letter of a sentence or the name of a day, Excel automatically converts the letter to uppercase.

**Tip**

### How can I delete an AutoCorrect entry?

**1** To delete an AutoCorrect entry, perform steps **1** and **2** on page 46 to display the AutoCorrect dialog box.

**2** Click the AutoCorrect entry you want to delete.

**3** Click **Delete** to remove the AutoCorrect entry from the list.

**4** Click **OK** to confirm your change.

---

**3** To add a new entry to the list, type the text you want Excel to replace automatically.

**4** Click this area and type the text you want Excel to automatically insert into your worksheets.

**5** Click **OK** to confirm your change.

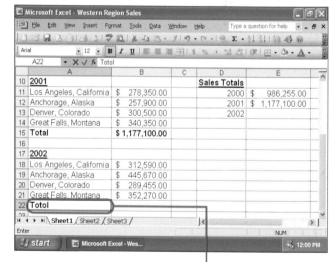

**INSERT AN AUTOCORRECT ENTRY**

■ After you create an AutoCorrect entry, Excel will automatically insert the entry each time you type the corresponding text.

**1** Type the text Excel will automatically replace and then press the **Spacebar** or Enter key.

■ Excel automatically replaces the text with the AutoCorrect entry.

# USING THE RESEARCH TASK PANE

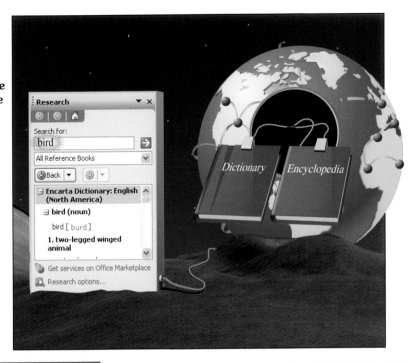

You can use the Research task pane to gather reference material without ever having to leave your Excel worksheet. For example, you can look up a word in a dictionary or search through an encyclopedia on the Web.

To use some of the resources offered in the Research task pane, your computer must be connected to the Internet.

Links to Web sites in the Research task pane that are preceded by a money icon (💵) require you to register and pay before you can view the information.

## USING THE RESEARCH TASK PANE

**1** Click 📖 to display the Research task pane.

■ The Research task pane appears.

**2** Click this area and type a word you want to research.

*Note: If this area contains text, drag the mouse I over the text to select the text before performing step 2.*

**3** Click this area to display a list of the resources you can use for your research.

**4** Click the resource you want to use to find information.

*Note: In this example, we select Encarta Encyclopedia. The following screens depend on the resource you select.*

**Tip**

**What types of resources can I search using the Research task pane?**

### Reference Books

You can choose to look up terms in reference books, such as the Encarta Dictionary or a thesaurus.

### Research Sites

You can research information online using eLibrary, Encarta Encyclopedia, Factiva News Search or MSN Search.

### Business and Financial Sites

You can access company and stock market information through Gale Company Profiles or MSN Money Stock Quotes. For information on inserting stock quotes, see page 62.

■ The reference material appears in this area.

■ Each word that appears in **bold** in this area offers information about the word you specified in step 2.

■ Below each **bold** word, a short description of the available information and one or more links that you can choose appear.

5 Click a link to view the information.

■ A Web browser window opens and displays the information you selected.

■ The Research task pane also appears in the Web browser window.

■ To research a different word at any time, double-click this area and type the word. Then press the Enter key.

6 To return to your document, click ✕.

# FIND DATA

You can use the Find feature to quickly locate every occurrence of a word or number in your worksheet.

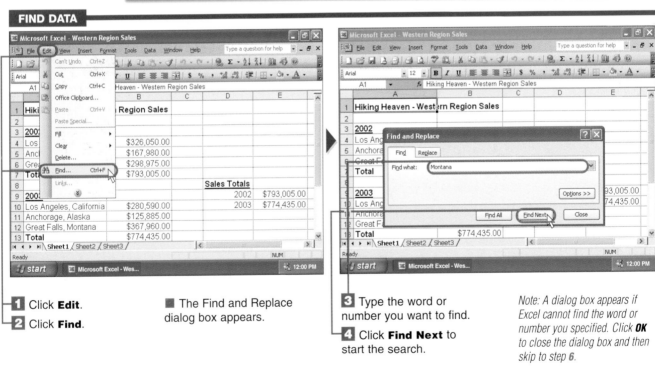

**1** Click **Edit**.

**2** Click **Find**.

■ The Find and Replace dialog box appears.

**3** Type the word or number you want to find.

**4** Click **Find Next** to start the search.

*Note: A dialog box appears if Excel cannot find the word or number you specified. Click **OK** to close the dialog box and then skip to step 6.*

### How will Excel search for the word or number I specify?

When you search for data in your worksheet, Excel will search for every instance of the data, even if the data appears in a formula or is part of a larger word or number. For example, if you search for the number 105, Excel will also find the numbers **105**.35, 2**105** and **105**6.

### Can I search only a specific section of my worksheet?

Yes. To search only a specific section of your worksheet, select the cells you want to search before starting the search. To select cells, see page 10.

■ Excel highlights the first cell containing the word or number.

*Note: If the Find and Replace dialog box covers a cell containing the word or number you want to find, Excel will automatically move the dialog box to a new location.*

**5** Click **Find Next** to find the next matching word or number. Repeat this step until you find the word or number you are searching for.

**6** To close the Find and Replace dialog box at any time, click **Close**.

# REPLACE DATA

You can find and replace every occurrence of a word or number in your worksheet. This is useful if you have incorrectly entered data throughout your worksheet.

## REPLACE DATA

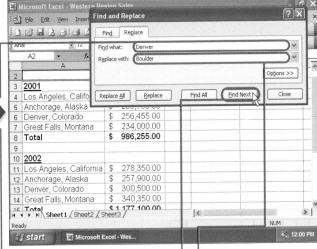

**1** Click **Edit**.

**2** Click **Replace**.

*Note: If Replace does not appear on the menu, position the mouse over the bottom of the menu to display the menu option.*

■ The Find and Replace dialog box appears.

**3** Type the word or number you want to replace with new data.

**4** Click this area and type the word or number you want to replace the data you typed in step **3**.

*Note: If the areas already contain data, drag the mouse I over the existing data and then type the word or number.*

**5** Click **Find Next** to start the search.

**Tip**

**Can Excel find and replace a number used in my formulas?**

Yes. Excel automatically searches the formulas in your worksheet for the number you specified. This is useful if you want to change a number used in several formulas. For example, if sales tax increases from 7% to 8%, you can search for all occurrences of **.07** in your formulas and replace them with **.08**.

**Tip**

**Can I use wildcard characters to find the data I want to replace?**

Yes. You can use an asterisk (*) or a question mark (?) to find the data you want to replace. The asterisk (*) represents one or more characters. The question mark (?) represents a single character. For example, type **Wend?** to find Wendi and Wendy.

■ Excel highlights the first cell containing the word or number you specified.

**6** Click one of these options.

**Replace All** - Replace all occurrences of the word or number in the worksheet.

**Replace** - Replace the word or number.

**Find Next** - Ignore the word or number.

*Note: To cancel the search at any time, press the* Esc *key.*

■ In this example, Excel replaces the word or number and searches for the next match.

*Note: If you selected Replace All in step 6, a dialog box appears, stating that the data was replaced. Click OK to close the dialog box and then skip to step 8.*

**7** Replace or ignore matching data until you find all the occurrences of the data you want to replace.

**8** Click **Close** to close the Find and Replace dialog box.

# LINK DATA

You can link data in one cell to another cell. When the data in the original cell changes, the linked data also changes.

Linking data is useful when you want cells to always display the same information. For example, you can link a formula in one cell to another cell in your worksheet. If the result of the formula changes, the linked cell will display the new result. For information on formulas, see pages 82 to 85.

## LINK DATA

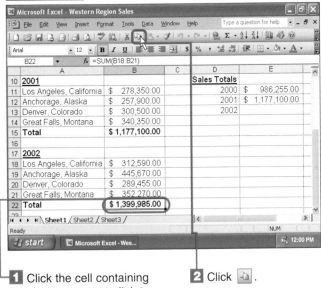

**1** Click the cell containing the data you want to link to another cell.

**2** Click 🗐.

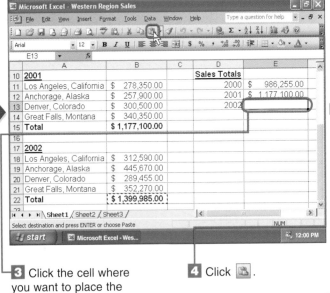

**3** Click the cell where you want to place the linked data.

**4** Click 🖺.

**Tip**

**Can I link data to a cell in another worksheet?**

Yes. You can link data to a cell in a different worksheet in the same workbook or a worksheet in another workbook. Perform steps **1** to **6** below, except switch to the worksheet you want to link the data to before performing step **3**. To switch between worksheets, see page 170. To switch between workbooks, see page 25.

**Tip**

**Can I move or delete the data in the original cell without affecting the link?**

When you move the data in the original cell, the link is not affected if the linked cell is in the same workbook. When you delete the data in the original cell, the linked cell displays a zero (0).

■ The Paste Options button appears in your worksheet.

**5** Click the Paste Options button to display a list of options.

**6** Click **Link Cells**.

*Note: The cell you are linking may not display the same data as the original cell until you perform step 6.*

■ The linked data appears in the cell.

■ The formula bar displays the location of the original cell.

■ To remove the moving border around the original cell, press the Esc key.

■ When the data in the original cell changes, the linked data also changes.

# NAME CELLS

You can give cells in your worksheet a meaningful name. Using named cells can save you time when selecting cells or entering formulas and functions.

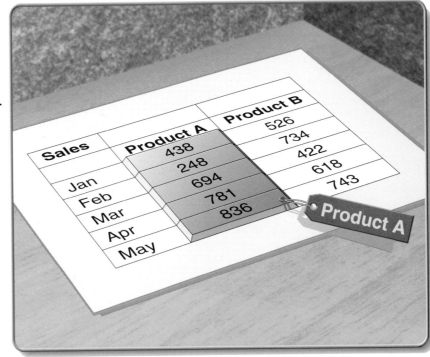

You can name a single cell or a range of cells in your worksheet.

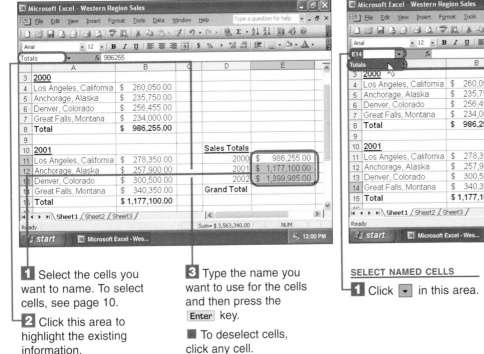

**1** Select the cells you want to name. To select cells, see page 10.

**2** Click this area to highlight the existing information.

**3** Type the name you want to use for the cells and then press the Enter key.

■ To deselect cells, click any cell.

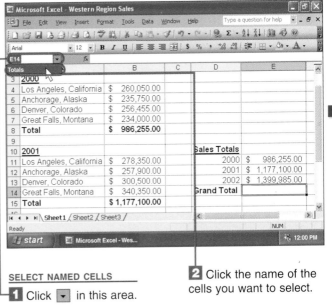

**SELECT NAMED CELLS**

**1** Click ▼ in this area.

**2** Click the name of the cells you want to select.

**Tip**

### What should I consider when naming cells?

You should consider the following guidelines when naming cells:

➤ Cell names can be up to 255 characters in length.

➤ Cell names must begin with either a letter or an underscore character ( _ ). The remaining characters can be any combination of letters, numbers, underscore characters or periods.

➤ Cell names cannot include spaces.

➤ Cell names cannot be a cell reference, such as **D4**.

➤ Cell names can contain both uppercase and lowercase letters.

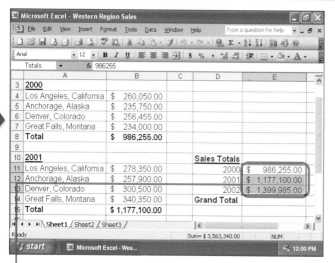

■ Excel highlights the cells in your worksheet.

**USING NAMED CELLS IN FORMULAS AND FUNCTIONS**

**Naming cells can make formulas and functions easier to enter and understand.**

■ In this example, we use cells named "Totals" in a function.

■ This cell contains the function **=SUM(Totals)** instead of the function **=SUM(E11:E13)**.

*Note: For information on formulas and functions, see pages 82 to 89.*

# ADD A COMMENT

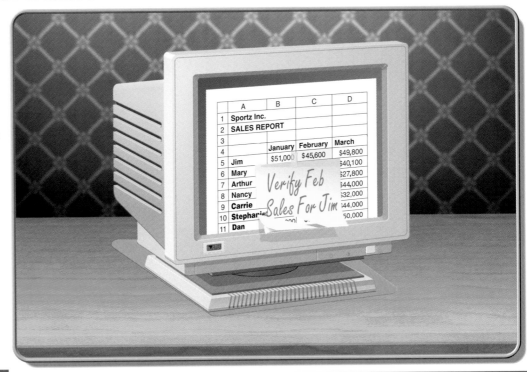

You can add a comment to a cell in your worksheet. A comment can be a note, explanation or reminder about data you need to verify later.

## ADD A COMMENT

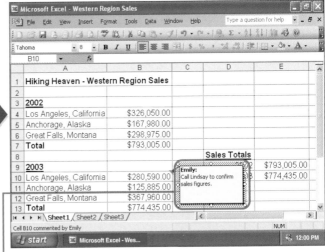

**1** Click the cell you want to add a comment to.

**2** Click **Insert**.

**3** Click **Comment**.

*Note: If Comment does not appear on the menu, position the mouse ⬡ over the bottom of the menu to display the menu option.*

■ A yellow comment box appears, displaying your name.

**4** Type the comment you want to add.

**5** When you finish typing your comment, click outside the comment box.

**Tip**

**How can I display all the comments in my worksheet at once?**

1 Click **View**.

2 Click **Comments**.

*Note: If Comments does not appear on the menu, position the mouse over the bottom of the menu to display the menu option.*

■ To once again hide the comments, repeat steps 1 and 2.

**Tip**

**Why didn't my comments print when I printed my worksheet?**

You must change the print options in Excel to specify that you want to print your comments. To change the print options, see page 156.

You can choose to print the comments on a separate page or as they are displayed in your worksheet. To print the comments as they are displayed in your worksheet, you must first display all the comments.

**Comments on a separate page**   **Comments in a worksheet**

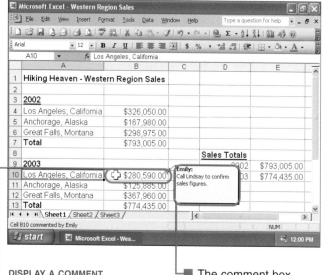

**DISPLAY A COMMENT**

■ A red triangle (◥) appears in a cell that contains a comment.

1 Position the mouse over the cell containing the comment you want to view.

■ The comment box appears, displaying the comment.

2 To hide the comment box, move the mouse outside the cell.

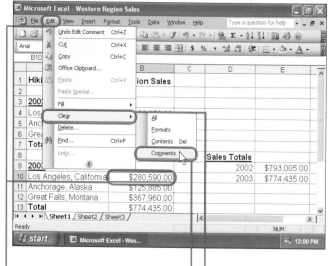

**DELETE A COMMENT**

1 Click the cell containing the comment you want to delete.

2 Click **Edit**.

3 Click **Clear**.

4 Click **Comments**.

■ The red triangle (◥) disappears from the cell.

59

# INSERT SYMBOLS

You can insert symbols that do not appear on your keyboard into your worksheet.

## INSERT SYMBOLS

**1** Click a cell in your worksheet where you want a symbol to appear.

**2** Click **Insert**.

**3** Click **Symbol**.

*Note: If Symbol does not appear on the menu, position the mouse ⬚ over the bottom of the menu to display the menu option.*

■ The Symbol dialog box appears, displaying the symbols for the current font.

**4** To display the symbols for another font, click ⬇ in this area.

**5** Click the font that provides the symbols you want to display.

**Tip**

**How can I quickly insert a symbol I recently used?**

**1** Perform steps 1 to 3 below to display the Symbol dialog box.

■ This area displays the most recently used symbols.

**2** Double-click the symbol you want to place in your worksheet.

**3** Click **Close** to close the Symbol dialog box.

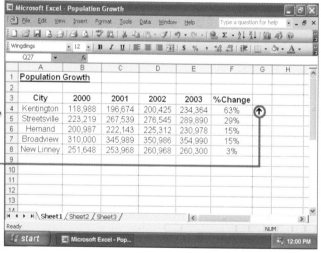

■ The symbols for the font you selected appear in this area.

**6** Click the symbol you want to place in your worksheet.

**7** Click **Insert** to insert the symbol into your worksheet.

**8** Click **Close** to close the Symbol dialog box.

■ The symbol appears in your worksheet.

■ To remove a symbol from your worksheet, double-click the cell displaying the symbol. Then drag the mouse I over the symbol until you highlight the symbol and press the Delete key.

# INSERT A STOCK QUOTE

You can use Excel's Research task pane to insert stock quotes into your worksheet.

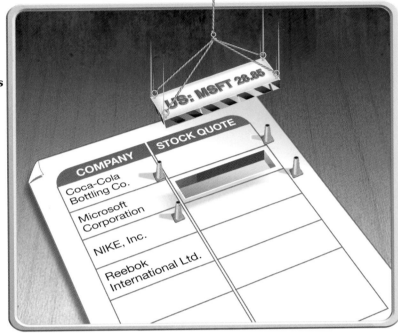

Excel allows you to access stock quotes through MSN Money Stock Quotes.

## INSERT A STOCK QUOTE

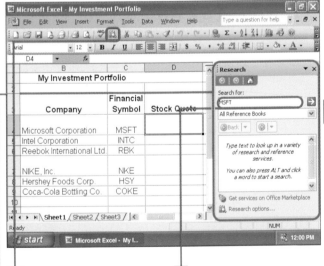

**1** Click 📖 to display the Research task pane.

■ The Research task pane appears.

**2** Click this area and type the financial symbol for the stock quote you want to find.

*Note: If this area contains text, drag the mouse I over the text to select the text before performing step 2.*

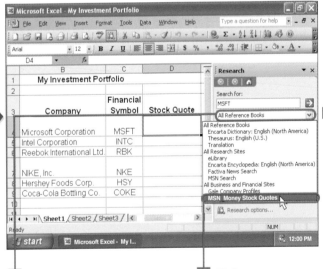

**3** Click this area to display a list of resources you can use to search for information.

**4** Click **MSN Money Stock Quotes**.

**Tip**

**How can I find the financial symbol of a company I want to insert a stock quote for?**

You can find financial symbols by using the stock symbol lookup tool available at the finance.yahoo.com/l Web site. The following is a list of financial symbols for some common companies.

| Company Name | Symbol |
|---|---|
| eBay Inc. | EBAY |
| FedEx Corporation | FDX |
| Goodyear Tire & Rubber | GT |
| Wal-Mart Stores Inc. | WMT |
| Wells Fargo & Company | WFC |

 **Tip**

**Can I access detailed information about a company of interest using the Research task pane?**

Yes. You can use Gale Company Profiles to find detailed company information. Perform steps **1** to **4** below, except select **Gale Company Profiles** in step **4**. Information such as the company's address, phone and fax numbers, number of employees and fiscal year end date appear in the Research task pane.

■ This area displays the stock quote information for the financial symbol you specified.

*Note: The displayed stock prices are delayed at least 20 minutes.*

**5** To insert the current stock quote into your worksheet, click the cell where you want the stock quote to appear.

**6** Click **Insert Price** to insert the stock quote into your worksheet.

■ The stock quote appears in the cell you selected.

■ You can repeat steps **2** to **6** to insert a stock quote for another company.

**7** To hide the Research task pane, click ☒.

## CHAPTER 4

# Work With Rows and Columns

*Are you wondering how to adjust, insert, delete or hide rows and columns in a worksheet? Read this chapter to find out how.*

# CHANGE COLUMN WIDTH

You can change the width of columns to improve the appearance of your worksheet and display any hidden data.

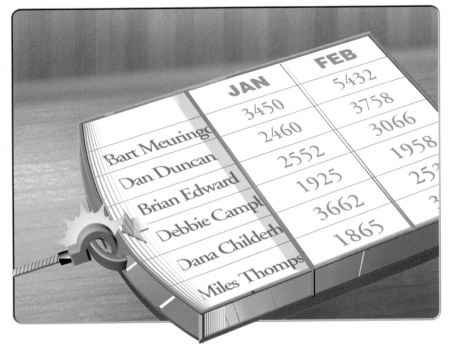

Data in a cell may be hidden if the cell is not wide enough to display the data and the neighboring cell also contains data. You can increase the column width to display all the data in the cell.

## CHANGE COLUMN WIDTH

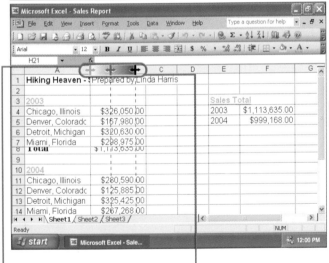

**1** To change the width of a column, position the mouse ⟨⟩ over the right edge of the column heading (⟨⟩ changes to ✛).

**2** Drag the column edge until the dashed line displays the column width you want.

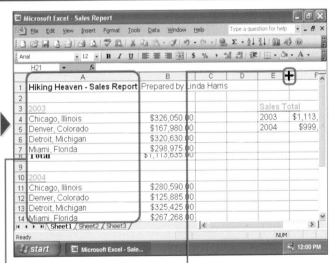

■ The column displays the new width.

### FIT LONGEST ITEM

**1** To change a column width to fit the longest item in the column, double-click the right edge of the column heading.

# CHANGE ROW HEIGHT

You can change the height of rows to add space between the rows of data in your worksheet.

## CHANGE ROW HEIGHT

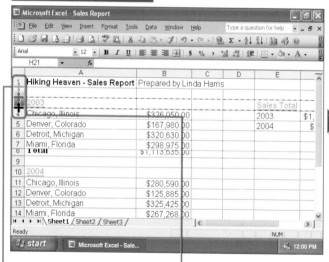

**1** To change the height of a row, position the mouse ⟨⟩ over the bottom edge of the row heading (⟨⟩ changes to +).

**2** Drag the row edge until the dashed line displays the row height you want.

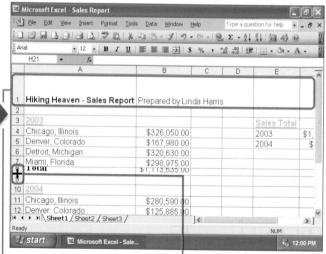

■ The row displays the new height.

### FIT TALLEST ITEM

**1** To change a row height to fit the tallest item in the row, double-click the bottom edge of the row heading.

# INSERT A ROW OR COLUMN

You can add a row or column to your worksheet to insert additional data.

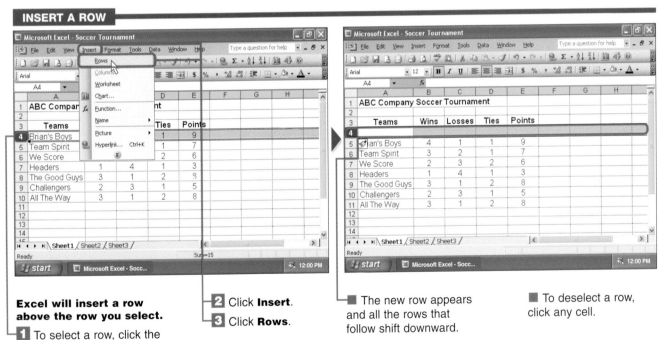

When you add a row or column, Excel automatically adjusts the row numbers and column letters in your worksheet for you.

## INSERT A ROW

**Excel will insert a row above the row you select.**

**1** To select a row, click the row number.

**2** Click **Insert**.

**3** Click **Rows**.

■ The new row appears and all the rows that follow shift downward.

■ To deselect a row, click any cell.

**Tip**

**Do I need to adjust my formulas when I insert a row or column?**

No. When you insert a row or column, Excel automatically updates any formulas affected by the insertion. For information on formulas, see pages 82 to 85.

**Tip**

**How do I insert several rows or columns at once?**

You can use one of the methods shown below to insert several rows or columns at once, but you must first select the number of rows or columns you want to insert. For example, to insert two columns, select two columns and then perform steps **2** and **3** below. To select multiple rows or columns, see page 11.

## INSERT A COLUMN

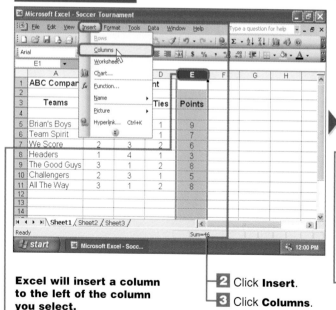

**Excel will insert a column to the left of the column you select.**

**1** To select a column, click the column letter.

**2** Click **Insert**.

**3** Click **Columns**.

■ The new column appears and all the columns that follow shift to the right.

■ To deselect a column, click any cell.

# DELETE A ROW OR COLUMN

You can delete a row or column to remove data you no longer want to display in your worksheet.

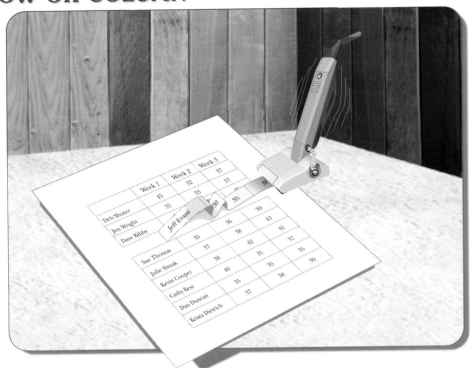

When you delete a row, the remaining rows in your worksheet shift upward. When you delete a column, the remaining columns shift to the left. Excel automatically adjusts the row numbers and column letters in your worksheet for you.

## DELETE A ROW

**1** To select the row you want to delete, click the row number.

**2** Click **Edit**.

**3** Click **Delete** to delete the row.

■ The row disappears and all the rows that follow shift upward.

■ To deselect a row, click any cell.

## Tip

**Why did #REF! appear in a cell after I deleted a row or column?**

If #REF! appears in a cell in your worksheet, you may have deleted data needed to calculate a formula. Before you delete a row or column, make sure the row or column does not contain data that is used in a formula. For information on formulas, see pages 82 to 85.

## Tip

**How do I delete several rows or columns at once?**

You can use one of the methods shown below to delete several rows or columns at once, but you must first select the rows or columns you want to delete. For example, to delete three columns, select the columns and then perform steps **2** and **3** below. To select multiple rows or columns, see page 11.

---

## DELETE A COLUMN

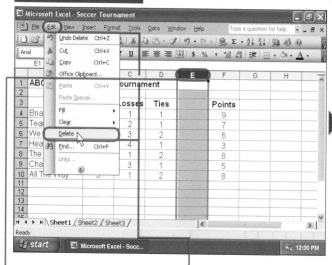

**1** To select the column you want to delete, click the column letter.

**2** Click **Edit**.

**3** Click **Delete** to delete the column.

■ The column disappears and all the columns that follow shift to the left.

■ To deselect a column, click any cell.

# INSERT CELLS

If you want to add new data to the middle of existing data in your worksheet, you can insert cells. The surrounding cells move to make room for the new cells.

INSERT CELLS

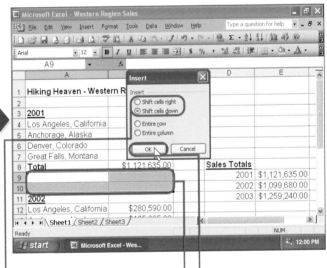

**1** Select the cells where you want to insert new cells. To select cells, see page 10.

*Note: Excel will insert the same number of cells as you select.*

**2** Click **Insert**.

**3** Click **Cells**.

*Note: If Cells does not appear on the menu, position the mouse ⟍ over the bottom of the menu to display the menu option.*

■ The Insert dialog box appears.

**4** Click an option to shift the surrounding cells to the right or down to make room for the new cells ( ○ changes to ◉ ).

**5** Click **OK** to insert the cells.

■ Excel inserts the new cells and shifts the surrounding cells in the direction you specified.

■ To deselect cells, click any cell.

# DELETE CELLS

You can remove cells you no longer need from your worksheet. The surrounding cells move to fill the empty space.

| | Income | Expenses | Profit |
|---|---|---|---|
| January | $ 245,000 | $ 203,345 | $ 41,655 |
| February | $ 245,995 | $ 199,900 | $ 75,990 |
| March | $ 250,000 | $ 210,700 | $ 28,400 |
| April | $ 275,890 | $ 210,445 | $ 10,540 |
| May | $ 239,100 | $ 207,600 | $ 6,190 |
| June | $ 220,985 | $ 209,200 | $ 26,470 |
| July | $ 213,790 | | |
| August | $ 235,670 | | |

## DELETE CELLS

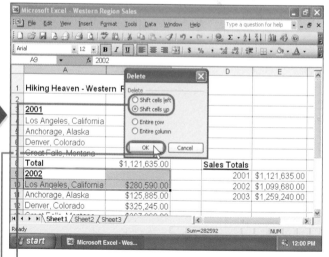

**1** Select the cells you want to delete. To select cells, see page 10.

**2** Click **Edit**.

**3** Click **Delete**.

■ The Delete dialog box appears.

**4** Click an option to shift the surrounding cells to the left or up to fill the empty space ( ○ changes to ◉ ).

**5** Click **OK** to delete the cells.

■ Excel removes the cells and shifts the surrounding cells in the direction you specified.

■ To deselect cells, click any cell.

73

# HIDE COLUMNS

You can hide columns in your worksheet to reduce the amount of data displayed on your screen or temporarily remove confidential data.

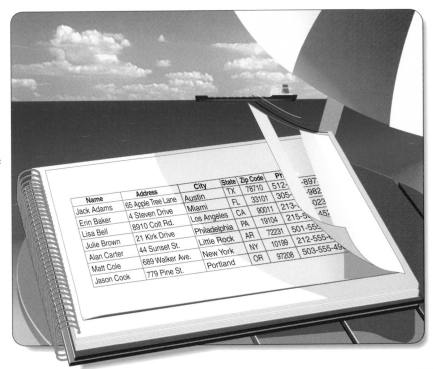

You can hide a single column or multiple columns in your worksheet.

Hidden columns will not appear when you print your worksheet. This allows you to produce a printed copy of your worksheet that does not include unneeded or confidential data.

## HIDE COLUMNS

**1** Select the columns you want to hide. To select columns, see page 11.

**2** Click **Format**.

**3** Click **Column**.

**4** Click **Hide** to hide the columns.

■ The columns you selected disappear from your worksheet.

■ To deselect cells, click any cell.

**Will hiding columns affect the formulas and functions in my worksheet?**

Hiding columns will not affect the results of formulas and functions in your worksheet. Excel will use data in the hidden columns to perform calculations even though the data is hidden from view. For information on formulas and functions, see pages 82 to 89.

**Can I hide rows in my worksheet?**

Yes. Select the rows you want to hide. To select rows, see page 11. Then perform steps **2** to **4** on page 74, selecting **Row** in step **3**. To display the hidden rows, select the rows directly above and below the hidden rows. Then perform steps **2** to **4** on page 75, selecting **Row** in step **3**.

**DISPLAY HIDDEN COLUMNS**

**1** Select the columns on each side of the hidden columns. To select columns, see page 11.

■ If the hidden column is the first column in the worksheet, click this area to select all the columns in the worksheet.

**2** Click **Format**.

**3** Click **Column**.

**4** Click **Unhide** to display the hidden columns.

■ The hidden columns reappear in your worksheet.

■ To deselect cells, click any cell.

# FREEZE ROWS AND COLUMNS

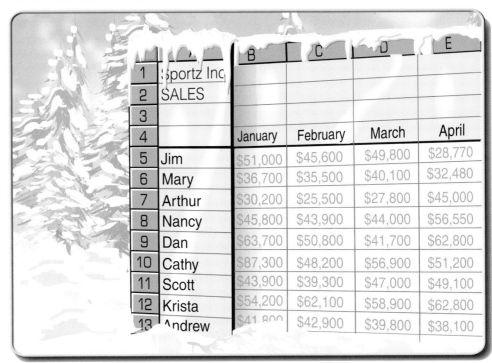

You can freeze rows and columns in your worksheet so they will not move. This allows you to keep row and column labels displayed on your screen as you move through a large worksheet.

FREEZE ROWS AND COLUMNS

Excel will freeze the rows above and the columns to the left of the cell you select.

**1** To select a cell, click the cell.

**2** Click **Window**.

**3** Click **Freeze Panes**.

**Tip**

## Can I freeze only rows or only columns in my worksheet?

Yes. To freeze only rows, select the row below the rows you want to freeze. To freeze only columns, select the column to the right of the columns you want to freeze. Then perform steps **2** and **3** below. To select a row or column, see page 11.

**Freeze Only Rows**   **Freeze Only Columns**

**Tip**

## How do I unfreeze rows and columns in my worksheet?

When you no longer want to keep rows and columns frozen on your screen, perform steps **2** and **3** below, selecting **Unfreeze Panes** in step **3**.

■ A horizontal line appears in your worksheet.

■ The rows above the horizontal line are frozen. These rows will remain on your screen as you move through your worksheet.

■ To move through the rows below the horizontal line, click ▲ or ▼.

■ A vertical line appears in your worksheet.

■ The columns to the left of the vertical line are frozen. These columns will remain on your screen as you move through your worksheet.

■ To move through the columns to the right of the vertical line, click ◄ or ►.

# SPLIT A WORKSHEET

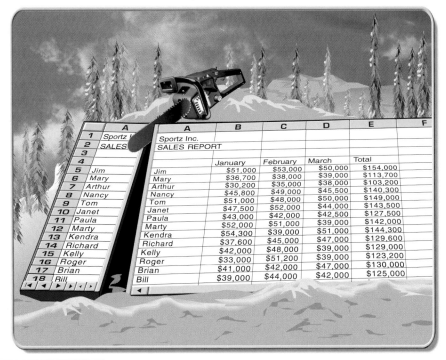

You can split your worksheet into separate sections. This allows you to display different areas of a large worksheet at the same time.

Each section of a split worksheet contains a copy of the entire worksheet.

## SPLIT A WORKSHEET VERTICALLY

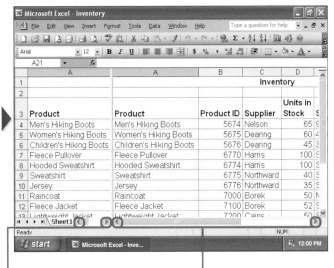

**1** Position the mouse 🔓 over this area (🔓 changes to ◀▐▶).

**2** Drag the mouse ◀▐▶ to where you want to split your worksheet.

■ The worksheet splits vertically into two sections.

■ To move through the columns to the left of the dividing line, click ◀ or ▶.

■ To move through the columns to the right of the dividing line, click ◀ or ▶.

**Tip**

**When I print a worksheet that is split into separate sections, will Excel print multiple copies of the worksheet?**

No. Excel will print the worksheet only once. The dividing line that splits your worksheet will not appear when you print the worksheet.

 **Tip**

**How do I remove a split from my worksheet?**

Position the mouse ⬚ over the dividing line in your worksheet (⬚ changes to ⬌ or ⬍). Then double-click the dividing line to remove the split.

## SPLIT A WORKSHEET HORIZONTALLY

**1** Position the mouse ⬚ over this area (⬚ changes to ⬍).

**2** Drag the mouse ⬍ to where you want to split your worksheet.

■ The worksheet splits horizontally into two sections.

■ To move through the rows above the dividing line, click ⬆ or ⬇.

■ To move through the rows below the dividing line, click ⬆ or ⬇.

## CHAPTER 5

# Work With Formulas and Functions

*Would you like to perform calculations on the data in your worksheet? Learn how in this chapter.*

# INTRODUCTION TO FORMULAS AND FUNCTIONS

**A formula allows you to calculate and analyze data in your worksheet.**

A formula always begins with an equal sign (=).

---

## OPERATORS

A formula can contain one or more operators. An operator specifies the type of calculation you want to perform.

### Arithmetic Operators

You can use arithmetic operators to perform mathematical calculations.

|   | A | B |
|---|---|---|
| 1 | 5 | 5 |
| 2 |   |   |
| 3 | 10 |   |

=A1+B1

| Operator | Description |
|----------|-------------|
| + | Addition (A1+B1) |
| - | Subtraction (A1-B1) |
| * | Multiplication (A1*B1) |
| / | Division (A1/B1) |
| % | Percent (A1%) |
| ^ | Exponentiation (A1^B1) |

### Comparison Operators

You can use comparison operators to compare two values. Comparison operators return a value of TRUE or FALSE.

|   | A | B |
|---|---|---|
| 1 | 5 | 5 |
| 2 |   |   |
| 3 | TRUE |   |

=A1=B1

| Operator | Description |
|----------|-------------|
| = | Equal to (A1=B1) |
| > | Greater than (A1>B1) |
| < | Less than (A1<B1) |
| >= | Greater than or equal to (A1>=B1) |
| <= | Less than or equal to (A1<=B1) |
| <> | Not equal to (A1<>B1) |

## ORDER OF CALCULATIONS

When a formula contains more than one operator, Excel performs the calculations in a specific order.

| | Order of Calculations |
|---|---|
| 1 | Percent (%) |
| 2 | Exponentiation (^) |
| 3 | Multiplication (*) and Division (/) |
| 4 | Addition (+) and Subtraction (-) |
| 5 | Comparison operators |

| | A |
|---|---|
| 1 | 2 |
| 2 | 4 |
| 3 | 6 |
| 4 | 8 |
| 5 | |
| 6 | |

=A1+A2+A3*A4
=2+4+6*8=54

=A1+(A2+A3)*A4
=2+(4+6)*8=82

=A1*(A3-A2)+A4
=2*(6-4)+8=12

=A2^A1+A3
=$4^2$+6=22

You can use parentheses ( ) to change the order in which Excel performs calculations. Excel will perform the calculations inside the parentheses first.

## CELL REFERENCES

When entering formulas, use cell references instead of actual data whenever possible. For example, enter the formula =A1+A2 instead of =10+20.

When you use cell references and you change a number used in a formula, Excel will automatically redo the calculation for you.

| | A | B |
|---|---|---|
| 1 | 10 | |
| 2 | 20 | |
| 3 | | |

=A1+A2= 30

## FUNCTIONS

A function is a ready-to-use formula that you can use to perform a calculation on the data in your worksheet. Examples of commonly used functions include AVERAGE, COUNT, MAX and SUM.

| | A |
|---|---|
| 1 | 10 |
| 2 | 20 |
| 3 | 30 |
| 4 | 40 |
| 5 | |
| 6 | |

=AVERAGE(A1:A4)
=(10+20+30+40)/4 = 25

=COUNT(A1:A4) = 4

=MAX(A1:A4) = 40

=SUM(A1:A4)
=10+20+30+40 = 100

■ A function always begins with an equal sign (=).

■ The data Excel will use to calculate a function is enclosed in parentheses ( ).

### Specify Individual Cells

When a comma (,) separates cell references in a function, Excel uses each cell to perform the calculation. For example, =SUM(A1,A2,A3) is the same as the formula =A1+A2+A3.

### Specify a Group of Cells

When a colon (:) separates cell references in a function, Excel uses the specified cells and all cells between them to perform the calculation. For example, =SUM(A1:A3) is the same as the formula =A1+A2+A3.

# ENTER A FORMULA

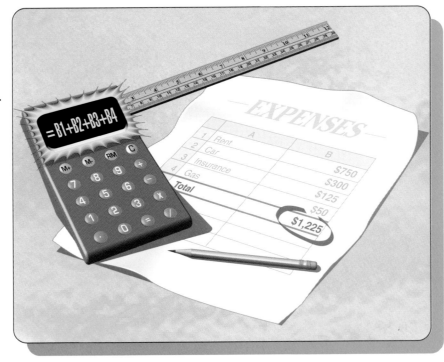

You can enter a formula into any cell in your worksheet. A formula helps you calculate and analyze data in your worksheet.

When entering formulas, you should use cell references instead of actual data whenever possible.

A formula always begins with an equal sign (=).

## ENTER A FORMULA

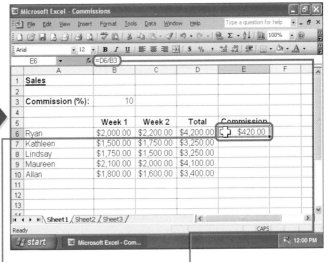

**1** Click the cell where you want to enter a formula.

**2** Type an equal sign (=) to begin the formula.

**3** Type the formula and then press the Enter key.

*Note: As you enter the formula, Excel adds a colored outline to each cell you refer to in the formula.*

■ The result of the calculation appears in the cell.

**4** To view the formula you entered, click the cell containing the formula.

■ The formula bar displays the formula for the cell.

## Tip

**What happens if I change a number used in a formula?**

When you use cell references and you change a number used in a formula, Excel will automatically redo the calculation for you.

## Tip

**How can I quickly enter cell references into a formula?**

To quickly enter cell references, perform steps **1** and **2** on page 84 and then click the first cell you want to use in the formula. Type the operator you want to use to perform the calculation and then click the next cell you want to use in the formula. When you finish entering cell references and operators, press the Enter key to perform the calculation.

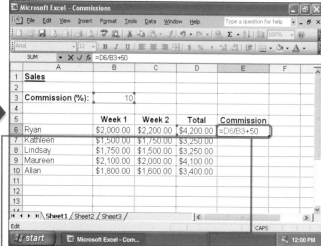

### EDIT A FORMULA

**1** Double-click the cell containing the formula you want to change.

■ The formula appears in the cell.

■ Excel outlines each cell used in the formula with a different color.

**2** Press the ← or → key to move the flashing insertion point to where you want to remove or add characters.

■ To remove the character to the left of the insertion point, press the •Backspace key.

**3** To add data where the insertion point flashes on your screen, type the data.

**4** When you finish making changes to the formula, press the Enter key.

# ENTER A FUNCTION

Excel helps you enter functions into your worksheet. Functions allow you to perform calculations without having to type long, complex formulas.

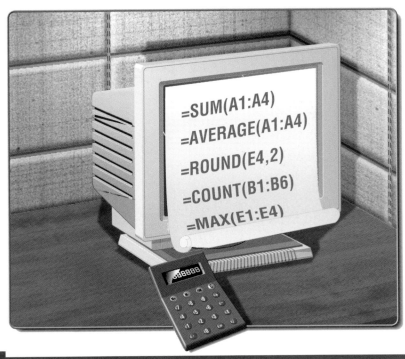

=SUM(A1:A4)
=AVERAGE(A1:A4)
=ROUND(E4,2)
=COUNT(B1:B6)
=MAX(E1:E4)

Excel offers over 200 functions to help you analyze data in your worksheet. There are financial functions, math and trigonometry functions, date and time functions, statistical functions and many more.

## ENTER A FUNCTION

**1** Click the cell where you want to enter a function.

**2** Click *fx* to enter a function.

■ The Insert Function dialog box appears.

**3** Click this area to display the categories of available functions.

**4** Click the category containing the function you want to use.

*Note: If you do not know which category contains the function you want to use, select **All** to display a list of all the functions.*

**Tip**

**Can Excel help me find
the function I should
use to perform a
calculation?**

If you do not know
which function to use to
perform a calculation,
you can have Excel
recommend a function.

**1** Perform steps **1** and **2**
below to display the Insert
Function dialog box.

**2** Type a brief description of
the calculation you want to
perform and then press the
Enter key.

■ This area displays a list of
recommended functions you
can use to perform the
calculation. You can perform
steps **5** to **11** below to use a
function Excel recommends.

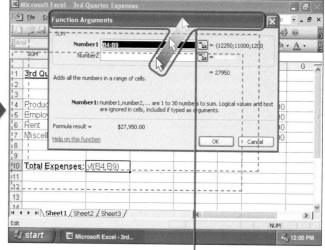

■ This area displays the
functions in the category
you selected.

**5** Click the function you
want to use.

■ This area describes
the function you selected.

**6** Click **OK** to continue.

■ The Function Arguments
dialog box appears. If the
dialog box covers data you
want to use in the function,
you can move the dialog
box to a new location.

**7** To move the dialog
box, position the mouse
over the title bar and then
drag the dialog box to a
new location.

**CONTINUED**

# ENTER A FUNCTION

When entering a function, you must specify which numbers you want to use in the calculation. You may need to specify several numbers or only one number, depending on the function you are using.

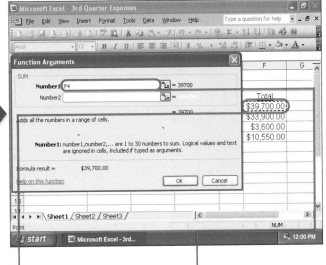

■ This area displays boxes where you enter the numbers you want to use in the function.

■ This area describes the numbers you need to enter.

**8** To enter the first number for the function, click the cell that contains the number.

*Note: If the number you want to use does not appear in your worksheet, type the number.*

■ The cell reference for the number appears in this area.

**Tip**

### Can I enter a function by myself?

If you know the name of the function you want to use, you can type the function and cell references directly into a cell in your worksheet. You must start the function with an equal sign (=), enclose the cell references in parentheses ( ) and separate each cell reference with a comma (,). You can also separate cell references with a colon (:) to indicate that Excel should include the specified cells and all the cells between them in the function.

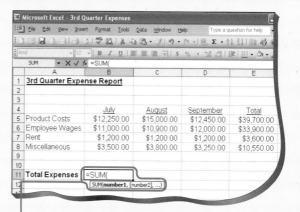

■ When you type a function directly into a cell, a yellow box appears, displaying the name of the function. You can click the name of the function to display help information about the function.

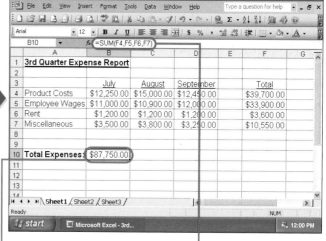

**9** To enter another number for the function, click the next box.

**10** Repeat steps **8** and **9** until you have entered all the numbers you want to use in the function.

**11** Click **OK** to enter the function into your worksheet.

■ The result of the function appears in the cell.

■ The formula bar displays the function for the cell.

# PERFORM COMMON CALCULATIONS

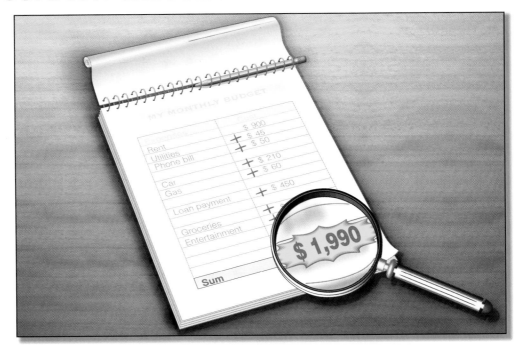

You can quickly perform common calculations on numbers in your worksheet. For example, you can calculate the sum of a list of numbers.

## PERFORM COMMON CALCULATIONS

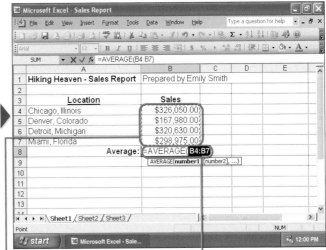

**1** Click the cell below or to the right of the cells containing the numbers you want to include in the calculation.

**2** Click ⏷ in this area to display a list of common calculations.

*Note: If* Σ ⏷ *is not displayed, click* ⏷ *on the Standard toolbar to display the button.*

**3** Click the calculation you want to perform.

*Note: If you want to quickly add the numbers, you can click* Σ *instead of performing steps 2 and 3.*

■ A moving outline appears around the cells that Excel will include in the calculation.

■ If Excel outlines the wrong cells, you can select the cells that contain the numbers you want to include in the calculation. To select cells, see page 10.

■ The cell you selected in step **1** displays the function Excel will use to perform the calculation.

**Tip**

### What common calculations can I perform?

| Sum | Adds a list of numbers. |
|-----|-------------------------|
| Average | Calculates the average value of a list of numbers. |
| Count | Calculates the number of values in a list. |
| Max | Finds the largest value in a list of numbers. |
| Min | Finds the smallest value in a list of numbers. |

**Tip**

### Can I perform calculations on several columns or rows of data at the same time?

Yes. Select the cells below or to the right of the cells that contain the numbers you want to include in the calculation. To select cells, see page 10. Then perform steps **2** and **3** below.

| | Product A | Product B | Month Totals |
|---|-----------|-----------|--------------|
| January | 10 | 5 | |
| February | 20 | 6 | |
| March | 30 | 3 | |

| | Product A | Product B | Month Totals |
|---|-----------|-----------|--------------|
| January | 10 | 5 | 15 |
| February | 20 | 6 | 26 |
| March | 30 | 3 | 33 |

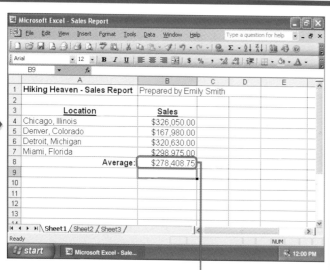

**4** Press the Enter key to perform the calculation.

■ The result of the calculation appears.

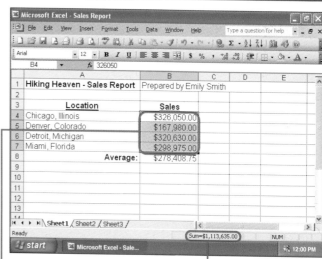

#### QUICKLY ADD NUMBERS

**You can quickly display the sum of a list of numbers without entering a formula into your worksheet.**

**1** Select the cells containing the numbers you want to add. To select cells, see page 10.

■ This area displays the sum of the cells you selected.

# COPY A FORMULA

If you want to use the same formula several times in your worksheet, you can save time by copying the formula.

| Feb | | |
|---|---|---|
| 2345 | 4343 | 3645 |
| 6543 | 7897 | 7249 |
| 3423 | 848 | 4562 |
| =B2+B3+B4 | =C2+C3+C4 | =D2+D3+D4 |

## COPY A FORMULA—USING RELATIVE REFERENCES

**1** Enter the formula you want to copy to other cells. To enter a formula, see page 84.

**2** Click the cell containing the formula you want to copy.

■ The formula bar displays the formula for the cell.

**3** Position the mouse ⛶ over the bottom right corner of the cell (⛶ changes to +).

**4** Drag the mouse + over the cells you want to receive a copy of the formula.

**Tip**

### What is a relative reference?

A relative reference is a cell reference that changes when you copy a formula.

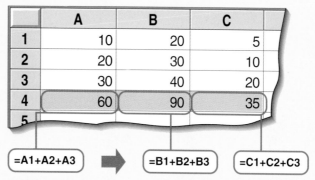

**=A1+A2+A3**

This cell contains the formula **=A1+A2+A3**.

**=B1+B2+B3**  **=C1+C2+C3**

When you copy the formula to other cells in your worksheet, Excel automatically changes the cell references in the new formulas.

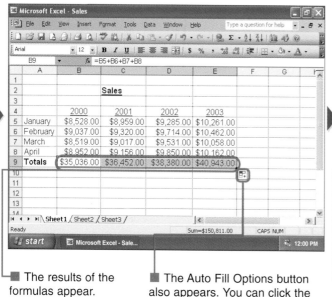

■ The results of the formulas appear.

■ The Auto Fill Options button also appears. You can click the button and then select an option to change the way Excel copies the formula. For example, you can specify that Excel should not use the formatting from the original cell.

**5** To view one of the new formulas, click a cell that received a copy of the formula.

■ The formula bar displays the formula with the new cell references.

**CONTINUED**

# COPY A FORMULA

You can copy a formula to other cells in your worksheet to save time. If you do not want Excel to change a cell reference when you copy a formula, you can use an absolute reference.

## COPY A FORMULA—USING ABSOLUTE REFERENCES

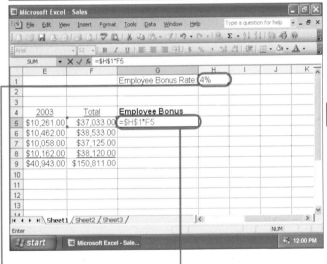

**1** Enter the data you want to use in all the formulas.

**2** Enter the formula you want to copy to other cells. To enter a formula, see page 84.

**3** Click the cell containing the formula you want to copy.

■ The formula bar displays the formula for the cell.

**4** Position the mouse ⛶ over the bottom right corner of the cell (⛶ changes to +).

**5** Drag the mouse + over the cells you want to receive a copy of the formula.

### Tip

**What is an absolute reference?**

An absolute reference is a cell reference that does not change when you copy a formula. To make a cell reference absolute, type a dollar sign ($) before both the column letter and row number, such as **$A$7**.

=$A$7*B2 ➡ =$A$7*C2    =$A$7*D2

This cell contains the formula =$A$7*B2.

When you copy the formula to other cells in your worksheet, Excel does not change the absolute reference in the new formulas.

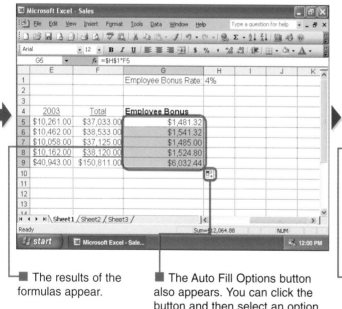

■ The results of the formulas appear.

■ The Auto Fill Options button also appears. You can click the button and then select an option to change the way Excel copies the formula. For example, you can specify that Excel should not use the formatting from the original cell.

**6** To view one of the new formulas, click a cell that received a copy of the formula.

■ The formula bar displays the formula with the absolute reference and the new cell reference.

# DISPLAY ALL FORMULAS

You can display the formulas in your worksheet instead of the results of the calculations.

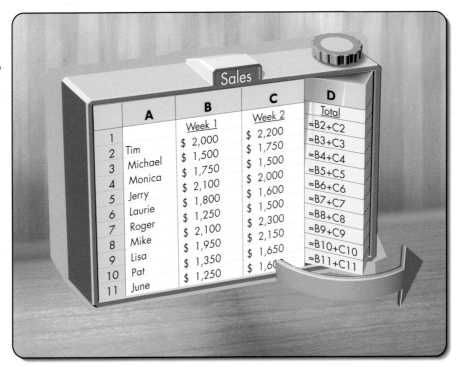

This is useful when you want to review or edit all the formulas in your worksheet.

## DISPLAY ALL FORMULAS

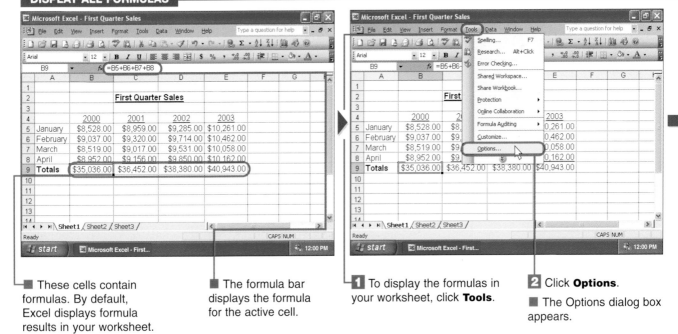

■ These cells contain formulas. By default, Excel displays formula results in your worksheet.

■ The formula bar displays the formula for the active cell.

**1** To display the formulas in your worksheet, click **Tools**.

**2** Click **Options**.

■ The Options dialog box appears.

**Tip**

**Why does the Formula Auditing toolbar appear when I display the formulas in my worksheet?**

The Formula Auditing toolbar contains buttons that you can use to work with the formulas in your worksheet. For example, you can click one of the following buttons to work with your formulas.

Checks errors in formulas and displays a dialog box that allows you to correct errors. For information on errors in formulas, see page 98.

Add a comment to a cell that contains a formula. For information on adding comments, see page 58.

**Tip**

**Is there another way to display the formulas in my worksheet?**

You can use the keyboard to switch between the display of formulas and formula results in your worksheet. To change the display at any time, press and hold down the Ctrl key and then press the ` key.

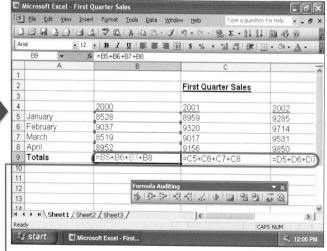

■ **3** Click the **View** tab.

■ **4** Click **Formulas** (☐ changes to ☑).

■ **5** Click **OK** to confirm your change.

■ The formulas appear in your worksheet.

■ Excel automatically adjusts the column widths to clearly display the formulas.

■ To once again show the formula results in your worksheet, repeat steps **1** to **5** (☑ changes to ☐ in step **4**).

# CHECK ERRORS IN FORMULAS

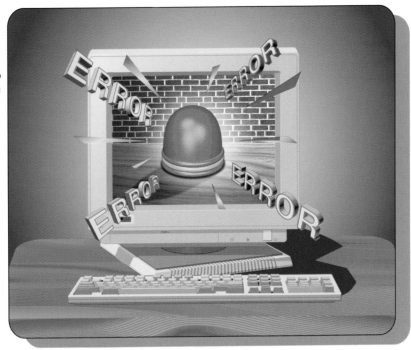

**Excel can help you determine the cause of an error in a formula.**

Excel checks your formulas for errors as you work and marks cells that display certain error messages. For information on common error messages, see page 99.

Errors in formulas are often the result of typing mistakes. Once you determine the cause of an error, you can edit the formula to correct the error. To edit a formula, see page 85.

CHECK ERRORS IN FORMULAS

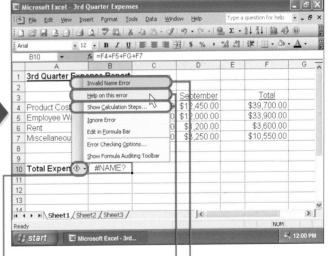

■ An error message appears in a cell when Excel cannot properly calculate the result of a formula.

■ A triangle appears in the top left corner of a cell that contains an error when Excel can help you determine the cause of the error.

■ **1** To determine the cause of an error, click a cell displaying a triangle.

■ The Error Checking button (◈) appears.

**2** Click the Error Checking button to display options you can use to determine the cause of the error.

■ This area displays the name of the error.

**3** You can click **Help on this error** to view help information for the error.

■ You can click **Show Calculation Steps** to have Excel help you evaluate the cause of the error.

## COMMON ERRORS IN FORMULAS

An error message appears when Excel cannot properly calculate or display the result of a formula.

**#####**

The column is too narrow to display the result of the calculation. You can change the column width to display the result. To change the column width, see page 66.

■ This cell contains the formula =A1*A2

**#DIV/0!**

The formula divides a number by zero (0). Excel considers a blank cell to have a value of zero.

■ This cell contains the formula =A1/A2
=50/0

**#NAME?**

The formula contains a function name or cell reference Excel does not recognize.

■ This cell contains the formula =AQ+A2+A3

In this example, the cell reference A1 was typed incorrectly.

**#REF!**

The formula refers to a cell that is not valid.

■ This cell contains the formula =A1+A2+A3

In this example, a row containing a cell used in the formula was deleted.

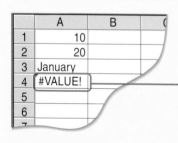

**#VALUE!**

The formula refers to a cell that Excel cannot use in a calculation.

■ This cell contains the formula =A1+A2+A3

In this example, a cell used in the formula contains text.

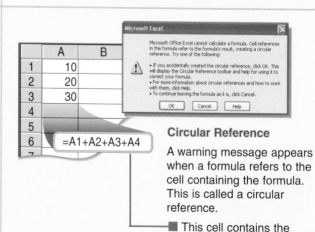

**Circular Reference**

A warning message appears when a formula refers to the cell containing the formula. This is called a circular reference.

■ This cell contains the formula =A1+A2+A3+A4

# CREATE SCENARIOS

A scenario is a set of alternate values for data in your worksheet. You can create multiple scenarios to see how different values affect your worksheet data.

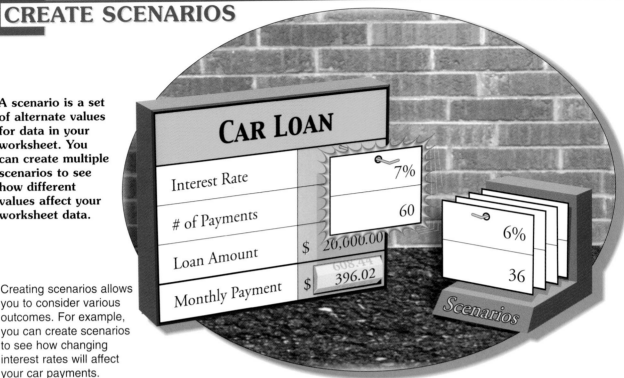

Creating scenarios allows you to consider various outcomes. For example, you can create scenarios to see how changing interest rates will affect your car payments.

## CREATE SCENARIOS

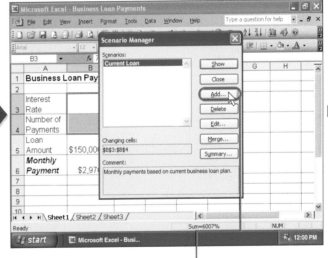

**1** Select the cells containing the data you want to change in the scenarios. To select cells, see page 10.

**2** Click **Tools**.

**3** Click **Scenarios**.

*Note: If Scenarios does not appear on the menu, position the mouse ⌖ over the bottom of the menu to display the menu option.*

■ The Scenario Manager dialog box appears.

**4** Click **Add** to create a new scenario.

**Tip**

### Should I save the original data as a scenario?

Yes. Excel will only keep the original data if you save the data as a scenario. You can use the scenario you create for the original data to redisplay the data at any time.

**Tip**

### What should I consider when entering a description for a scenario?

The description you enter for a scenario should clearly explain the purpose of the scenario. This will help you easily distinguish the scenario from other scenarios you create.

■ The Add Scenario dialog box appears.

**5** Type a name for the scenario you want to create.

**6** To enter a description for the scenario, drag the mouse I over the text in this area until you highlight the text. Then type a description.

**7** Click **OK** to continue.

■ The Scenario Values dialog box appears.

■ These areas display the original data in the cells you selected.

■ To save the original data as a scenario, skip to step **9** on page 102.

CONTINUED

# CREATE SCENARIOS

Excel saves your scenarios with your worksheet. You can display a different scenario at any time.

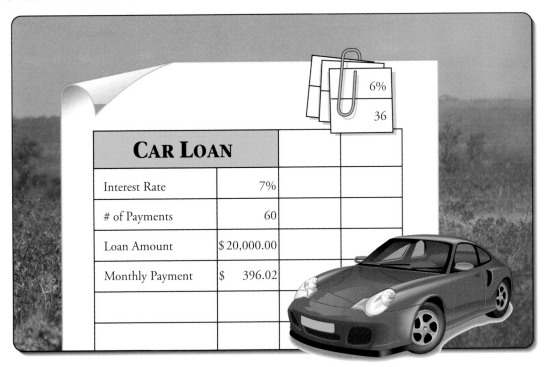

| CAR LOAN | | |
|---|---|---|
| Interest Rate | 7% | |
| # of Payments | 60 | |
| Loan Amount | $ 20,000.00 | |
| Monthly Payment | $ 396.02 | |
| | | |
| | | |

## CREATE SCENARIOS (CONTINUED)

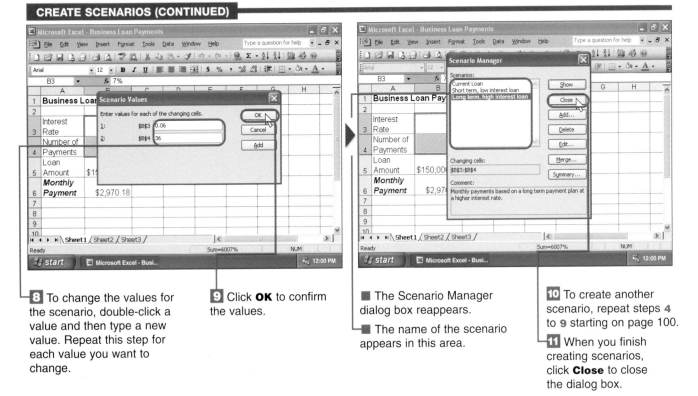

**8** To change the values for the scenario, double-click a value and then type a new value. Repeat this step for each value you want to change.

**9** Click **OK** to confirm the values.

■ The Scenario Manager dialog box reappears.

■ The name of the scenario appears in this area.

**10** To create another scenario, repeat steps **4** to **9** starting on page 100.

**11** When you finish creating scenarios, click **Close** to close the dialog box.

**Tip**

**How can I move the Scenario Manager dialog box so it is not covering the data in my worksheet?**

To move the Scenario Manager dialog box, position the mouse ⌖ over the title bar and then drag the dialog box to a new location.

**Tip**

**How do I delete a scenario I no longer need?**

**1** Perform steps **2** and **3** on page 100 to display the Scenario Manager dialog box.

**2** Click the scenario you want to delete.

**3** Click **Delete** to delete the scenario.

---

**DISPLAY A SCENARIO**

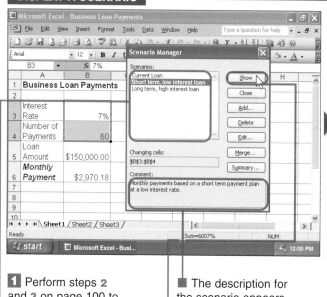

**1** Perform steps **2** and **3** on page 100 to display the Scenario Manager dialog box.

■ This area lists the scenarios you created.

**2** Click the scenario you want to display.

■ The description for the scenario appears in this area.

**3** Click **Show** to display the scenario in your worksheet.

■ Excel replaces the data in your worksheet with the values you entered for the scenario.

■ Any formulas that use the data update automatically.

■ You can repeat steps **2** and **3** to display other scenarios.

**4** When you finish displaying scenarios, click **Close** to close the dialog box.

■ The data from the last scenario you displayed remains in your worksheet.

# CREATE A SCENARIO SUMMARY REPORT

You can create a summary report to display the values for each scenario and the effects of the scenarios on the calculations in your worksheet.

Summary reports are useful when you want to quickly review or print the results of all the scenarios you created.

## CREATE A SCENARIO SUMMARY REPORT

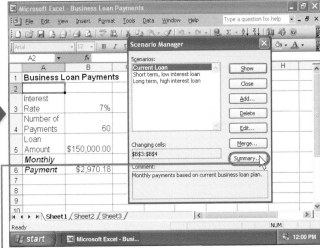

**1** Click **Tools**.

**2** Click **Scenarios**.

*Note: If Scenarios does not appear on the menu, position the mouse over the bottom of the menu to display the menu option.*

■ The Scenario Manager dialog box appears.

**3** Click **Summary** to create a summary report.

■ The Scenario Summary dialog box appears.

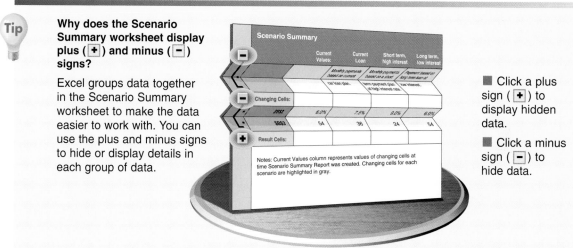

**Why does the Scenario Summary worksheet display plus ( + ) and minus ( – ) signs?**

Excel groups data together in the Scenario Summary worksheet to make the data easier to work with. You can use the plus and minus signs to hide or display details in each group of data.

■ Click a plus sign ( + ) to display hidden data.

■ Click a minus sign ( – ) to hide data.

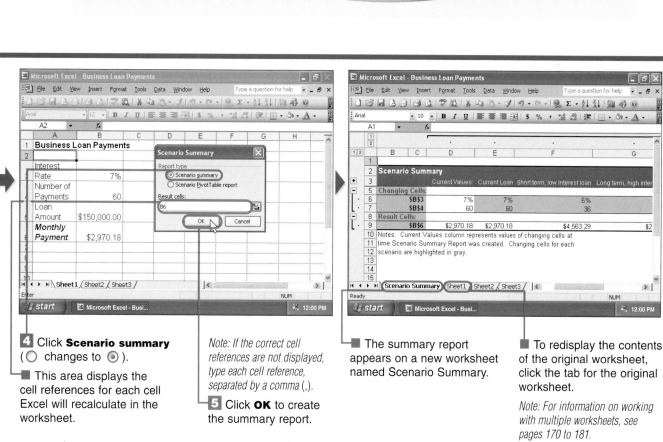

4 Click **Scenario summary** ( ○ changes to ◉ ).

■ This area displays the cell references for each cell Excel will recalculate in the worksheet.

*Note: If the correct cell references are not displayed, type each cell reference, separated by a comma (,).*

5 Click **OK** to create the summary report.

■ The summary report appears on a new worksheet named Scenario Summary.

■ To redisplay the contents of the original worksheet, click the tab for the original worksheet.

*Note: For information on working with multiple worksheets, see pages 170 to 181.*

**Central Division Standings**

| Pool A | Games | Goals | Wins | Losses | Ties | Points |
|---|---|---|---|---|---|---|
| Walt's Winners | 6 | 15 | 4 | 1 | 1 | 9 |
| The Chargers | 6 | 13 | 3 | 2 | 1 | 7 |
| Terry's Tigers | 6 | 12 | 3 | 3 | 0 | 6 |
| The Breakaways | 6 | 10 | 1 | 3 | 2 | 4 |
| The GO Team | 6 | 9 | 1 | 4 | 1 | 3 |

| Pool B | Games | Goals | Wins | Losses | Ties | Points |
|---|---|---|---|---|---|---|
| | | 15 | 4 | 1 | 1 | 9 |
| | | 13 | 3 | 1 | 2 | 8 |
| | | | 4 | 2 | 0 | 8 |
| | | | 3 | 3 | 0 | 6 |
| | | | 1 | 3 | 2 | 4 |
| | | | 1 | 5 | 0 | 2 |

## CHAPTER 6

# Change Your Screen Display

*Are you interested in changing the way your worksheet appears on your screen? In this chapter, you will learn how to zoom in and out, move toolbars and more.*

# ZOOM IN OR OUT

**You can enlarge or reduce the display of data on your screen.**

Changing the zoom setting allows you to see data in more detail or display more data on your screen at once. Changing the zoom setting will not affect the way data appears on a printed page.

## ZOOM IN OR OUT

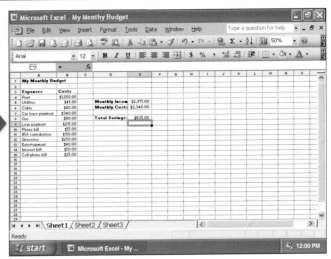

**1** Click ⬝ in this area to display a list of zoom settings.

*Note: If the Zoom area is not displayed, click ⬝ on the Standard toolbar to display the area.*

**2** Click the zoom setting you want to use.

*Note: If you select cells before performing step 1, the **Selection** setting enlarges the selected cells to fill the window. To select cells, see page 10.*

■ The worksheet appears in the new zoom setting. You can edit the worksheet as usual.

■ To return to the normal zoom setting, repeat steps 1 and 2, selecting **100%** in step 2.

# DISPLAY FULL SCREEN

You can display a
larger working area
by hiding parts of
the Excel screen.

Using the full
screen to view
a worksheet is
useful if you want
to display as many
cells as possible
while you review
and edit a large
worksheet.

## DISPLAY FULL SCREEN

**1** Click **View**.

**2** Click **Full Screen**.

*Note: If Full Screen does not
appear on the menu, position
the mouse ⤢ over the bottom
of the menu to display the
menu option.*

■ Excel hides parts of the
screen to display a larger
working area.

■ To once again display the
hidden parts of the screen,
click **Close Full Screen**.

*Note: You can also repeat
steps 1 and 2 to once again
display the hidden parts of
the screen.*

# DISPLAY OR HIDE THE STATUS BAR

You can display or hide the status bar at any time. The status bar displays information about the tasks you perform in Excel.

## DISPLAY OR HIDE THE STATUS BAR

**1** Click **View**.

■ A check mark (✔) appears beside Status Bar if the bar is currently displayed.

**2** Click **Status Bar** to display or hide the bar.

*Note: If Status Bar does not appear on the menu, position the mouse ⍦ over the bottom of the menu to display the menu option.*

■ Excel displays or hides the status bar.

*Note: Hiding the status bar provides a larger and less cluttered working area.*

# DISPLAY OR HIDE A TOOLBAR

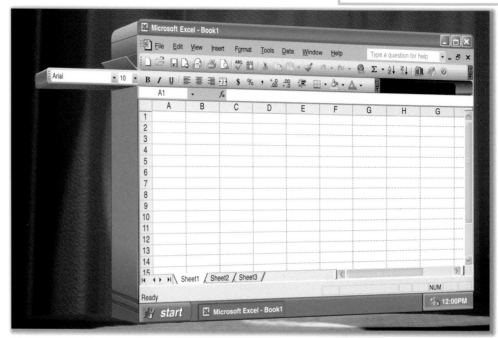

**Excel offers several toolbars that you can display or hide to suit your needs. Toolbars contain buttons that you can select to quickly perform common tasks.**

When you first start Excel, the Standard and Formatting toolbars appear on your screen.

## DISPLAY OR HIDE A TOOLBAR

■ **1** Click **View**.

■ **2** Click **Toolbars**.

■ A list of toolbars appears. A check mark (✔) appears beside the name of each toolbar that is currently displayed.

■ **3** Click the name of the toolbar you want to display or hide.

■ Excel displays or hides the toolbar you selected.

*Note: A screen displaying fewer toolbars provides a larger and less cluttered working area.*

111

# MOVE A TOOLBAR

You can move a toolbar to the top, bottom, right or left edge of your screen.

You can move a toolbar to the same row as another toolbar or to its own row.

MOVE A TOOLBAR

**1** Position the mouse over the left edge of the toolbar you want to move (changes to ✛).

**2** Drag the toolbar to a new location.

■ The toolbar appears in the new location.

# RESIZE A TOOLBAR

You can increase the size of a toolbar to display more buttons on the toolbar. This is useful when a toolbar appears on the same row as another toolbar and cannot display all of its buttons.

You cannot resize a toolbar that appears on its own row.

## RESIZE A TOOLBAR

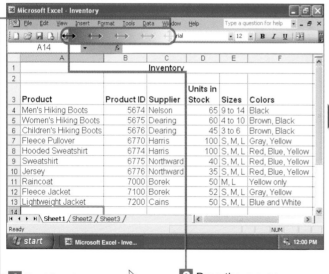

**1** Position the mouse over the left edge of the toolbar you want to resize (changes to ✛ ).

**2** Drag the mouse ↔ until the toolbar is the size you want.

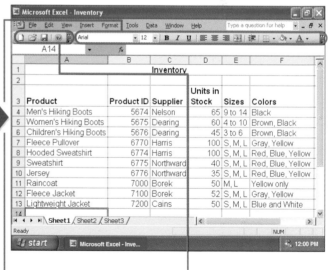

■ The toolbar displays the new size.

■ The new toolbar size affects the size of other toolbars on the same row.

| | Jan | Feb | Mar | Total |
|---|---|---|---|---|
| East | 7 | 7 | 5 | 19 |
| West | 6 | 4 | 7 | 17 |
| South | 8 | 7 | 9 | 24 |
| Total | 21 | 18 | 21 | 60 |

**Bold** *Italic* <u>Underline</u>

## CHAPTER 7

# Format Your Worksheets

*Would you like to improve the appearance of your worksheet? This chapter shows you how to change the color of data, add borders to cells and much more.*

# CHANGE FONT OF DATA

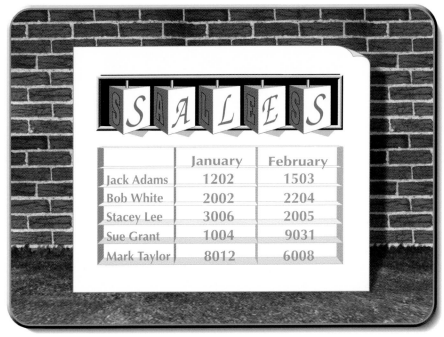

You can change the font of data to enhance the appearance of your worksheet.

By default, Excel uses the Arial font. You can use another font to draw attention to headings or emphasize important data in your worksheet.

**CHANGE FONT OF DATA**

**1** Select the cells containing the data you want to change to a different font. To select cells, see page 10.

**2** Click ⌄ in this area to display a list of the available fonts.

*Note: If the Font area is not displayed, click ⌄ on the Formatting toolbar to display the area.*

**3** Click the font you want to use.

■ The data changes to the font you selected.

■ To deselect cells, click any cell.

# CHANGE SIZE OF DATA

You can increase
or decrease the
size of data in
your worksheet.

Larger data is
easier to read,
but smaller data
allows you to fit
more information
on a page.

Excel measures
the size of data in
points. There are
approximately 72
points in one inch.

## CHANGE SIZE OF DATA

**1** Select the cells
containing the data you
want to change to a
new size. To select
cells, see page 10.

**2** Click ⋅ in this area
to display a list of the
available sizes.

*Note: If the Font Size area is
not displayed, click ⋅ on the
Formatting toolbar to display
the area.*

**3** Click the size you
want to use.

■ The data changes to
the size you selected.

■ To deselect cells, click
any cell.

117

# CHANGE FONT FOR ALL NEW WORKBOOKS

You can change the font that Excel uses for all new workbooks you create. This is useful when you want all your future workbooks to appear in a specific font.

## CHANGE FONT FOR ALL NEW WORKBOOKS

**1** Click **Tools**.

**2** Click **Options**.

■ The Options dialog box appears.

**3** Click the **General** tab.

**4** To select the font you want to use for all your new workbooks, click ⌄ in this area.

**5** Click the font you want to use.

**Tip**

**Will changing the font for all new workbooks affect the data in the workbooks I have already created?**

No. Excel will not change the font or size of data in the workbooks you have already created. To change the font or size of data in existing workbooks, see page 116 or 117.

**Tip**

**What parts of my workbooks will be affected when I change the font for all new workbooks?**

In addition to the data in your workbooks, the row numbers, column letters and data displayed in the formula bar will appear in the new font and size.

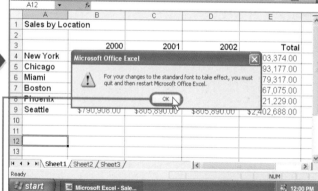

**6** To select the font size you want to use for all your new workbooks, click ⌄ in this area.

**7** Click the font size you want to use.

**8** Click **OK** to confirm your changes.

■ A dialog box appears, stating that you must exit Excel and restart the program for the changes to take effect.

**9** Click **OK** to continue.

■ You must now exit and restart Excel to use the font in new workbooks you create. To exit and restart Excel, see page 4.

# BOLD, ITALICIZE OR UNDERLINE DATA

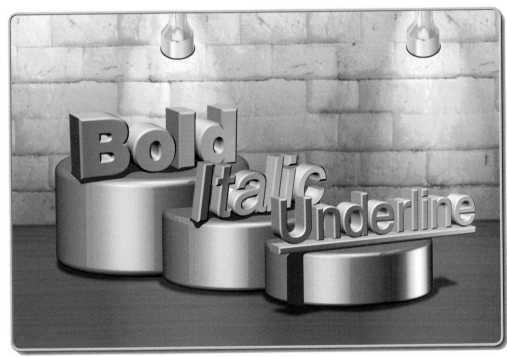

You can bold, italicize or underline data to emphasize data and enhance the appearance of your worksheet.

## BOLD, ITALICIZE OR UNDERLINE DATA

**1** Select the cells containing the data you want to bold, italicize or underline. To select cells, see page 10.

**2** Click one of the following buttons.

**B** Bold

*I* Italic

**U** Underline

Note: If the button you want is not displayed, click on the Formatting toolbar to display the button.

■ The data appears in the style you selected.

■ To deselect cells, click any cell.

■ To remove a bold, italic or underline style, repeat steps **1** and **2**.

You can align data
in different ways
to enhance the
appearance of
your worksheet.

When you enter
data into cells, Excel
automatically left
aligns text and right
aligns numbers and
dates.

## CHANGE HORIZONTAL ALIGNMENT OF DATA

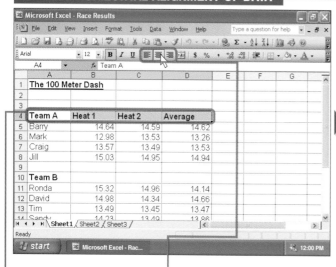

**1** Select the cells
containing the data
you want to align
differently. To select
cells, see page 10.

**2** Click one of the following
buttons.

≡ Left align

≡ Center

≡ Right align

*Note: If the button you want is not
displayed, click ░ on the Formatting
toolbar to display the button.*

■ The data appears in
the new alignment.

■ To deselect cells, click
any cell.

# CHANGE VERTICAL ALIGNMENT OF DATA

You can change the way Excel positions data between the top and bottom edges of a cell in your worksheet. This is useful for emphasizing row and column labels.

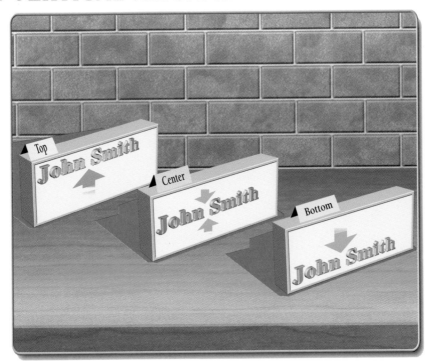

When you enter data into a cell, Excel automatically aligns the data at the bottom of the cell.

The most commonly used vertical alignment options are top, center, and bottom.

CHANGE VERTICAL ALIGNMENT OF DATA

**1** Select the cells containing the data you want to align differently. To select cells, see page 10.

**2** Click **Format**.

**3** Click **Cells**.

■ The Format Cells dialog box appears.

**Tip**

**Is there another way I can emphasize row and column labels?**

Yes. You can rotate data to emphasize row and column labels.

**1** Perform steps **1** to **4** starting on page 122.

**2** Position the mouse ↖ over the line in this area and then drag the line to a new angle.

**3** Click **OK** to confirm your change.

*Note: Excel will automatically change the row height to fit the rotated data.*

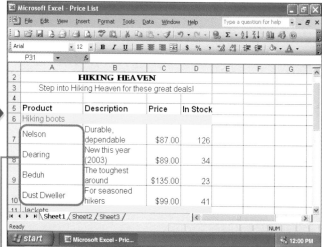

**4** Click the **Alignment** tab.

**5** Click this area to select the way you want to align the data.

**6** Click the way you want to align the data.

**7** Click **OK** to confirm your change.

■ The data displays the new alignment.

*Note: If the data does not display the new alignment, you may need to increase the height of the row. To change the row height, see page 67.*

■ To deselect cells, click any cell.

**123**

# CHANGE APPEARANCE OF DATA

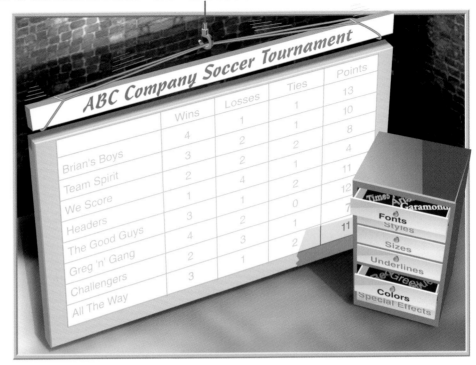

You can make data in your worksheet look more attractive by using various fonts, styles, sizes, effects and underlines.

## CHANGE APPEARANCE OF DATA

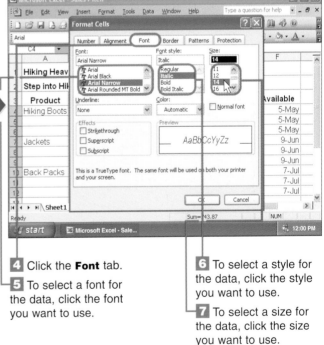

**1** Select the cells containing the data you want to change. To select cells, see page 10.

**2** Click **Format**.

**3** Click **Cells**.

■ The Format Cells dialog box appears.

**4** Click the **Font** tab.

**5** To select a font for the data, click the font you want to use.

**6** To select a style for the data, click the style you want to use.

**7** To select a size for the data, click the size you want to use.

**Tip**

**What determines which fonts are available on my computer?**

The fonts available on your computer depend on the programs installed on your computer. You can obtain additional fonts at computer stores and on the Internet.

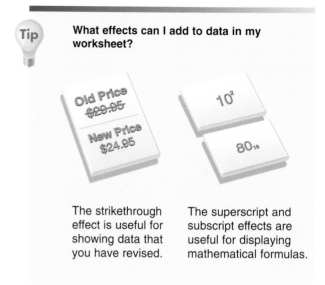

**Tip**

**What effects can I add to data in my worksheet?**

The strikethrough effect is useful for showing data that you have revised.

The superscript and subscript effects are useful for displaying mathematical formulas.

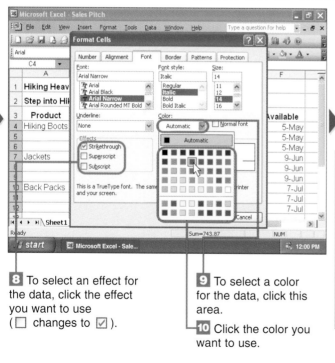

**8** To select an effect for the data, click the effect you want to use ( □ changes to ☑ ).

**9** To select a color for the data, click this area.

**10** Click the color you want to use.

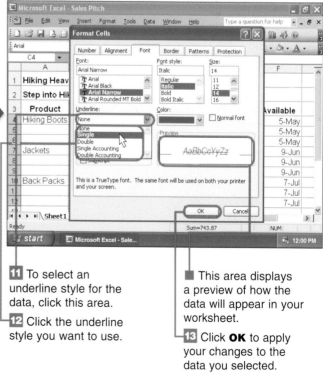

**11** To select an underline style for the data, click this area.

**12** Click the underline style you want to use.

■ This area displays a preview of how the data will appear in your worksheet.

**13** Click **OK** to apply your changes to the data you selected.

# CHANGE DATA COLOR

You can change the color of data in your worksheet to draw attention to headings or important information.

Adding color to data is also useful for marking data you want to review or verify later.

## CHANGE DATA COLOR

**1** Select the cells containing the data you want to change to a different color. To select cells, see page 10.

**2** Click ⬝ in this area to display the available colors.

*Note: If ⚊ is not displayed, click ⚊ on the Formatting toolbar to display the button.*

**3** Click the color you want to use.

■ The data appears in the color you selected.

■ To deselect cells, click any cell.

■ To return data to its original color, repeat steps **1** to **3**, selecting **Automatic** in step **3**.

126

# CHANGE CELL COLOR

**You can add color to cells to make the cells stand out in your worksheet.**

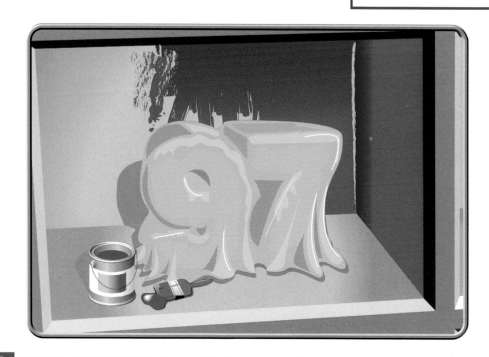

Changing the color of cells is useful when you want to distinguish between different areas in your worksheet. For example, in a worksheet that contains monthly sales figures, you can use a different cell color for each month.

## CHANGE CELL COLOR

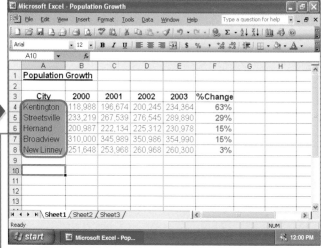

**1** Select the cells you want to change to a different color. To select cells, see page 10.

**2** Click ▾ in this area to display the available colors.

*Note: If ⬛▾ is not displayed, click ⬛ on the Formatting toolbar to display the button.*

**3** Click the color you want to use.

■ The cells appear in the color you selected.

■ To deselect cells, click any cell.

■ To remove color from cells, repeat steps 1 to 3, selecting **No Fill** in step 3.

# INDENT DATA

You can indent data to move the data away from the left edge of a cell.

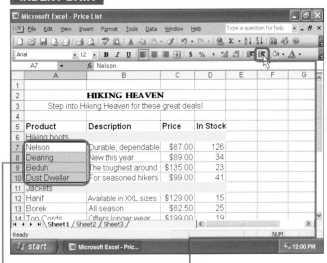

**1** Select the cells containing the data you want to indent. To select cells, see page 10.

**2** Click 📑 to indent the data.

*Note: If 📑 is not displayed, click ⁞⁞ on the Formatting toolbar to display the button.*

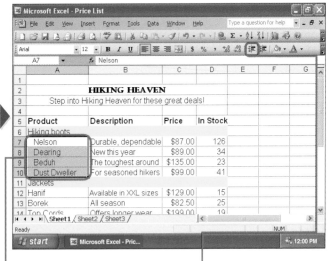

■ Excel indents the data.

■ You can repeat step **2** to further indent the data.

■ To decrease the indent, click 📑 .

*Note: If 📑 is not displayed, click ⁞⁞ on the Formatting toolbar to display the button.*

■ To deselect cells, click any cell.

128

# CENTER DATA ACROSS COLUMNS

You can center data across columns in your worksheet. This is useful for centering titles over your data.

## CENTER DATA ACROSS COLUMNS

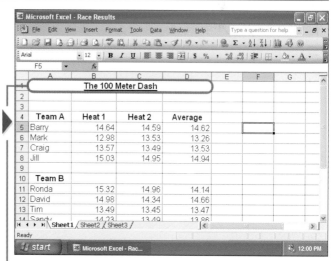

**1** Select the cells you want to center the data across. To select cells, see page 10.

*Note: The first cell you select should contain the data you want to center.*

**2** Click ▦ to center the data across the columns.

*Note: If ▦ is not displayed, click ▪ on the Formatting toolbar to display the button.*

■ Excel centers the data across the columns.

■ If you no longer want to center the data across the columns, click the cell that contains the data and then repeat step **2**.

# WRAP TEXT IN CELLS

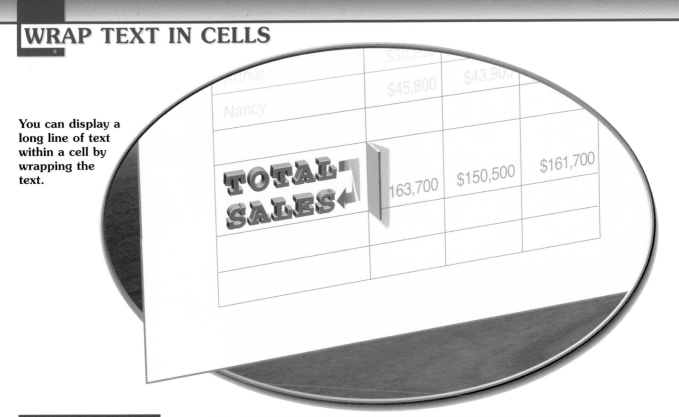

You can display a
long line of text
within a cell by
wrapping the
text.

## WRAP TEXT IN CELLS

**1** Select the cells containing
the text you want to wrap.
To select cells, see page 10.

**2** Click **Format**.

**3** Click **Cells**.

■ The Format Cells
dialog box appears.

**Tip**

**Can I display all the text in a cell without wrapping the text?**

You can have Excel reduce the size of text to fit within a cell. Perform steps **1** to **6** below, selecting **Shrink to fit** in step **5** (☐ changes to ☑ ).

If you later change the width of the column, Excel will automatically adjust the size of the text to fit the new width.

**Tip**

**Can I wrap text when entering text into a cell?**

Yes. Type the text you want to display on the first line of the cell. Then press and hold down the Alt key as you press the Enter key to wrap to the next line. You can then type the text for the next line. You may need to increase the column width to properly see where the text wraps. To change the column width, see page 66.

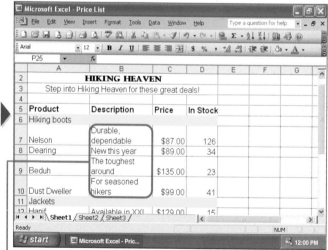

**4** Click the **Alignment** tab.

**5** Click **Wrap text** (☐ changes to ☑ ).

**6** Click **OK** to confirm your change.

■ The text wraps within the cells you selected.

■ Excel automatically adjusts the row heights to fit the wrapped text.

■ To deselect cells, click any cell.

# ADD BORDERS TO CELLS

You can add borders to cells to enhance the appearance of your worksheet.

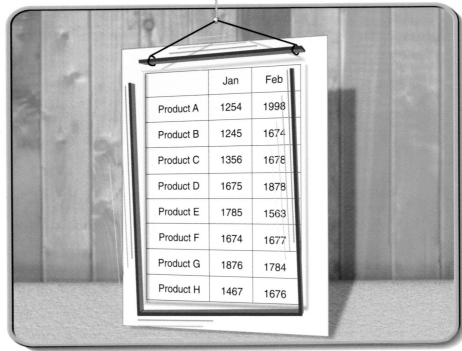

| | Jan | Feb |
|---|---|---|
| Product A | 1254 | 1998 |
| Product B | 1245 | 1674 |
| Product C | 1356 | 1678 |
| Product D | 1675 | 1878 |
| Product E | 1785 | 1563 |
| Product F | 1674 | 1677 |
| Product G | 1876 | 1784 |
| Product H | 1467 | 1676 |

Adding borders to cells is also useful if you want to divide your worksheet into sections.

## ADD BORDERS TO CELLS

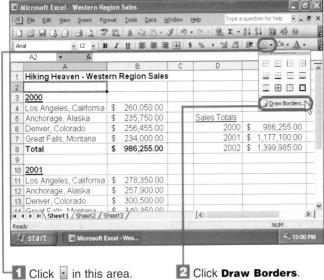

**1** Click ⬝ in this area.

**2** Click **Draw Borders**.

■ The Borders toolbar appears.

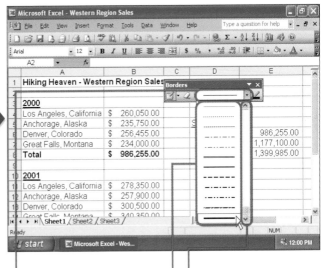

**3** To select a line style for the border, click this area.

■ You can use the scroll bar to browse through the available line styles.

**4** Click the line style you want to use.

**Tip**

**How can I quickly add borders to cells in my worksheet?**

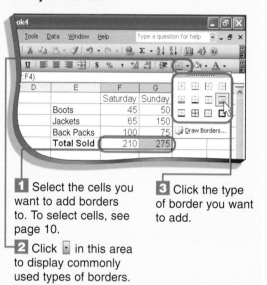

**1** Select the cells you want to add borders to. To select cells, see page 10.

**2** Click ⋅ in this area to display commonly used types of borders.

**3** Click the type of border you want to add.

**Tip**

**How do I remove borders from cells?**

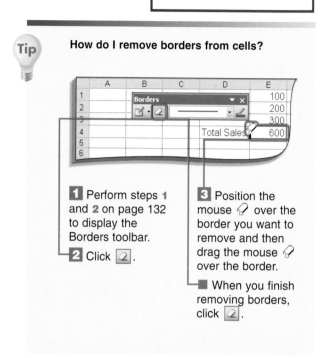

**1** Perform steps **1** and **2** on page 132 to display the Borders toolbar.

**2** Click 🖉.

**3** Position the mouse 🖉 over the border you want to remove and then drag the mouse 🖉 over the border.

■ When you finish removing borders, click 🖉.

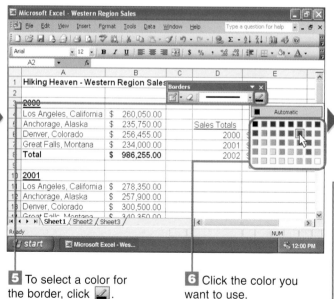

**5** To select a color for the border, click 🖊.

**6** Click the color you want to use.

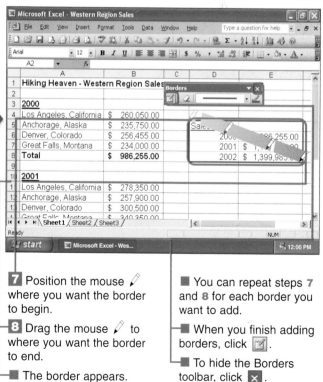

**7** Position the mouse 🖉 where you want the border to begin.

**8** Drag the mouse 🖉 to where you want the border to end.

■ The border appears.

■ You can repeat steps **7** and **8** for each border you want to add.

■ When you finish adding borders, click 🖉.

■ To hide the Borders toolbar, click ✕.

**133**

# CHANGE NUMBER FORMAT

You can change the appearance of numbers in your worksheet without retyping the numbers.

When you change the format of numbers, you do not change the value of the numbers.

**CHANGE NUMBER FORMAT**

**1** Select the cells containing the numbers you want to format. To select cells, see page 10.

**2** Click **Format**.

**3** Click **Cells**.

■ The Format Cells dialog box appears.

**4** Click the **Number** tab.

**5** Click the category that describes the numbers in the cells you selected.

■ This area displays the options for the category you selected. The available options depend on the category you selected.

**Tip**

## What categories are available for formatting numbers?

| Category: | Description: | Example: |
|---|---|---|
| General | Applies no specific number format. | 100 |
| Number | Used to format numbers for general display. | 100.00 |
| Currency | Used to format monetary values. | $100.00 |
| Accounting | Aligns the currency symbols and decimal points in a column of monetary values. | $ 100.00 <br> $ 1200.00 |
| Date | Used to format dates. | 23-Apr-03 |
| Time | Used to format times. | 12:00 PM |
| Percentage | Used to format percentages. | 25.00% |
| Fraction | Used to format fractions. | 1/4 |
| Scientific | Used to format numbers in scientific notation. | 1.00E+02 |
| Text | Treats numbers as text. | 135 Hillcrest Street |
| Special | Used to format special numbers, such as Zip codes. | 90210 |
| Custom | Allows you to apply your own number format. | 3-45-678 |

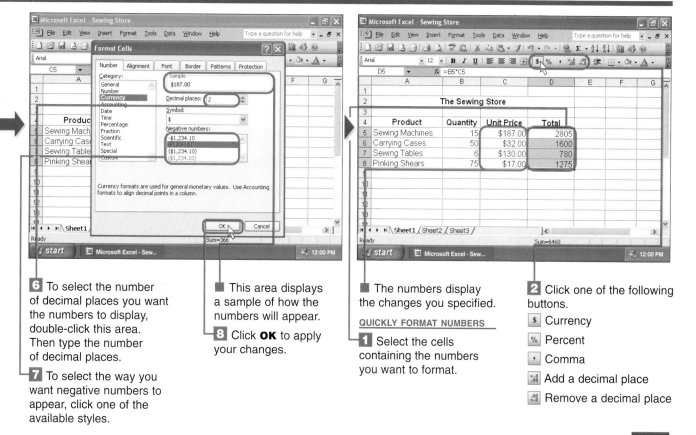

■6 To select the number of decimal places you want the numbers to display, double-click this area. Then type the number of decimal places.

■7 To select the way you want negative numbers to appear, click one of the available styles.

■ This area displays a sample of how the numbers will appear.

■8 Click **OK** to apply your changes.

■ The numbers display the changes you specified.

**QUICKLY FORMAT NUMBERS**

■1 Select the cells containing the numbers you want to format.

■2 Click one of the following buttons.

$ Currency

% Percent

, Comma

Add a decimal place

Remove a decimal place

# COPY FORMATTING

You can copy the formatting of a cell to make other cells in your worksheet look exactly the same.

You may want to copy the formatting of cells to make all the titles in your worksheet look the same. This will give the information in your worksheet a consistent appearance.

## COPY FORMATTING

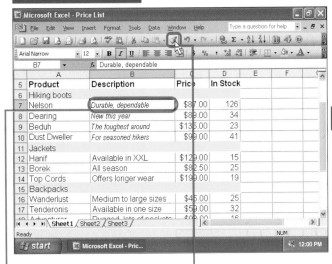

**1** Click a cell that displays the formatting you want to copy to other cells.

**2** Click ✍ to copy the formatting of the cell.

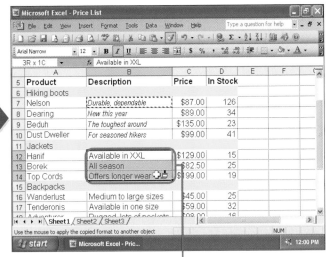

■ The mouse ⊕ changes to ⊕🖌 when over your worksheet.

**3** Select the cells you want to display the formatting. To select cells, see page 10.

**Tip**

## What types of formatting can I copy?

### Number Formatting

Number formatting can include currency, percentage and date formats.

### Data Formatting

Data formatting can include the font, size, color and alignment of data.

### Cell Formatting

Cell formatting can include borders and colors.

$6,000,000.00

**Tip**

## How can I remove the formatting from cells?

**1** Select the cells you want to remove the formatting from. To select cells, see page 10.

**2** Click **Edit**.

**3** Click **Clear**.

**4** Click **Formats**.

*Note: If you remove the formatting from cells containing dates, the dates change to numbers. To once again display the dates, you must change the format of the cells to the Date format. For more information, see page 134.*

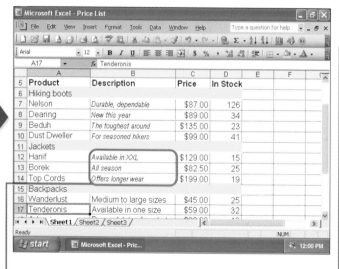

■ The cells you selected display the formatting.

■ To deselect cells, click any cell.

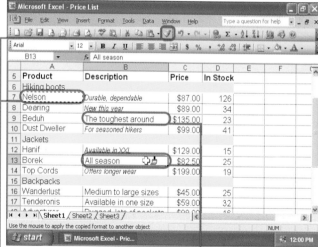

**COPY FORMATTING
TO SEVERAL AREAS**

**1** Click a cell that displays the formatting you want to copy to other cells.

**2** Double-click 🖌 to copy the formatting of the cell.

**3** Select each group of cells you want to display the formatting.

**4** When you finish copying the formatting, press the Esc key.

# APPLY AN AUTOFORMAT

Excel offers many ready-to-use designs that you can choose from to give your worksheet a professional appearance.

## APPLY AN AUTOFORMAT

**1** Select the cells you want to format. To select cells, see page 10.

**2** Click **Format**.

**3** Click **AutoFormat**.

■ The AutoFormat dialog box appears.

■ This area displays the available autoformats.

■ You can use the scroll bar to browse through the available autoformats.

**4** Click the autoformat you want to use.

**5** To view the formatting options for the autoformats, click **Options**.

## What formatting will Excel apply to the cells in my worksheet?

Each autoformat includes a combination of formats, such as fonts, colors, borders, alignments and number styles. When you apply an autoformat, Excel may also adjust the column width and row height of the cells to best fit the data in the cells.

## What happens if I add data to my worksheet after applying an autoformat?

If you enter data directly to the right or below the cells you applied an autoformat to, Excel may automatically format the new data. If Excel does not automatically format the new data, you can select all the cells you want to display the autoformat and then perform steps **2** to **7** below.

■ The formatting options appear in this area. A check mark (✔) beside an option indicates that Excel will apply the option to the cells.

**6** You can click an option to add ( ☑ ) or remove ( ☐ ) a check mark.

**7** Click **OK** to apply the autoformat to the cells you selected.

■ The cells display the autoformat you selected.

■ To deselect cells, click any cell.

■ To remove an autoformat, repeat steps **1** to **4**, selecting **None** in step **4**. Then perform step **7**.

# APPLY CONDITIONAL FORMATTING

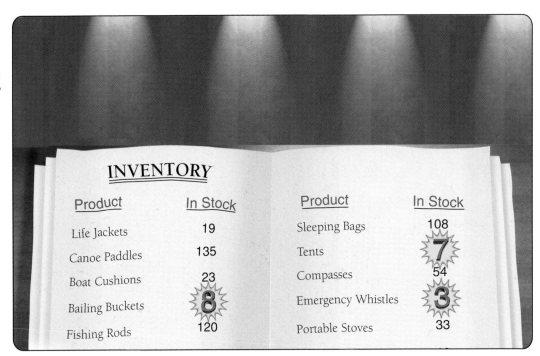

You can have Excel apply formatting to data when the data meets a condition you specify. This can help you quickly locate important data on a large worksheet.

For example, when the number of units in stock falls below 10, you can have Excel display the number in red.

## APPLY CONDITIONAL FORMATTING

**1** Select the cells containing the data you want Excel to format when the data meets a condition. To select cells, see page 10.

**2** Click **Format**.

**3** Click **Conditional Formatting**.

■ The Conditional Formatting dialog box appears.

**4** Click this area to select an operator for the condition.

**5** Click the operator you want to use.

**What is an operator?**

An operator tells Excel how to compare the data in a cell to the value you specify for a condition. For example, you can use the **greater than** operator when you want Excel to determine whether the data in a cell has a value of more than 100.

**6** Click this area and type the value you want to use for the condition.

**7** If you selected **between** or **not between** in step **5**, click this area and type the second value.

**8** Click **Format** to specify how you want to format the data when the data meets the condition.

■ The Format Cells dialog box appears.

CONTINUED

# APPLY CONDITIONAL FORMATTING

You can specify a color and style for data that meets the condition you specified.

**9** To select a color for the data, click this area to display the available colors.

**10** Click the color you want to use.

**11** To select a style for the data, click the style you want to use.

■ This area displays a preview of the options you selected.

**12** Click **OK** to confirm your changes.

**Tip**

**What happens if data no longer meets the condition I specified?**

If data no longer meets the condition, Excel will remove the conditional formatting from the data, but will not remove the condition from the cell. If data in the cell meets the condition in the future, Excel will apply the conditional formatting to the data.

**Tip**

**Can I copy conditional formatting?**

Yes. Copying conditional formatting is useful when you want other cells in your worksheet to display the same formatting under the same conditions. You can copy conditional formatting as you would copy any formatting in your worksheet. To copy formatting, see page 136.

■ This area displays how data that meets the condition will appear in your worksheet.

**13** Click **OK** to apply the condition to the cells you selected.

■ The data in the cells you selected displays the formatting if the data meets the condition you specified.

■ To deselect cells, click any cell.

**REMOVE CONDITIONAL FORMATTING**

**1** To remove conditional formatting from cells, perform steps **1** to **4** on the top of page 137 to clear the formatting.

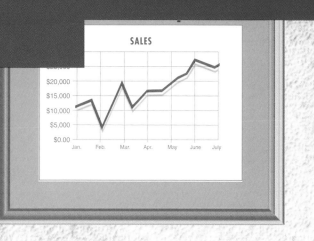

## CHAPTER 8

# Print Your Worksheets

*Are you ready to print your worksheet? In this chapter, you will learn how to preview your worksheet before printing and change the way your worksheet appears on a printed page.*

# PREVIEW A WORKSHEET BEFORE PRINTING

You can use the
Print Preview
feature to see how
your worksheet will
look when printed.
This allows you to
confirm that the
worksheet will print
the way you expect.

## PREVIEW A WORKSHEET BEFORE PRINTING

**1** Click 🔍 to preview
your worksheet before
printing.

*Note: If 🔍 is not displayed,
click ▪ on the Standard
toolbar to display the button.*

■ The Print Preview
window appears.

■ This area displays
a page from your
worksheet.

■ This area indicates
which page is displayed
and the total number of
pages in your worksheet.

**2** If your worksheet
contains more than one
page, you can click **Next**
or **Previous** to view the
next or previous page.

■ You can also use the
scroll bar to view other
pages.

**Tip**

**Why does my worksheet appear in black and white in the Print Preview window?**

If you are using a black-and-white printer, your worksheet appears in black and white in the Print Preview window. If you are using a color printer, your worksheet will appear in color.

**Tip**

**Why don't the gridlines appear on my worksheet in the Print Preview window?**

By default, Excel will not print the gridlines that appear around each cell in your worksheet. To print gridlines and change other print options, see page 156.

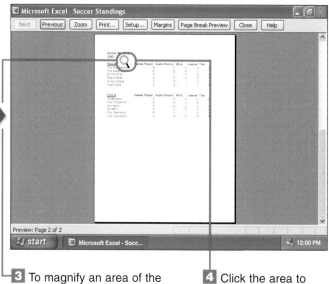

**3** To magnify an area of the page, position the mouse over the area you want to magnify (changes to Q).

**4** Click the area to magnify the area.

■ A magnified view of the area appears.

**5** To once again display the entire page, click anywhere on the page.

**6** When you finish previewing your worksheet, click **Close** to close the Print Preview window.

# PRINT A WORKSHEET

You can produce a
paper copy of the
worksheet displayed
on your screen.
Printing a worksheet
is useful when you
want to be able
to refer to the
worksheet without
using your computer.

Before printing your
worksheet, make sure
your printer is turned
on and contains paper.

## PRINT A WORKSHEET

**1** Click any cell in the
worksheet you want to print.

■ To print only specific cells
in your worksheet, select the
cells you want to print. To
select cells, see page 10.

**2** Click **File**.

**3** Click **Print**.

■ The Print dialog
box appears.

**4** Click the part of the
workbook you want to
print ( ○ changes to ● ).

*Note: For information on
the parts of the workbook
that you can print, see the
top of page 149.*

**5** If the part of the workbook
you selected to print contains
more than one page, click an
option to specify which pages
you want to print ( ○ changes
to ● ).

**All** - Prints every page

**Page(s)** - Prints the pages
you specify

## Tip

### What parts of a workbook can I print?

Excel allows you to specify which part of a workbook you want to print. Each workbook is divided into several worksheets.

For information on using multiple worksheets in a workbook, see pages 170 to 181.

**Selection**

Prints the cells you selected.

**Active sheet(s)**

Prints the displayed worksheet.

**Entire workbook**

Prints every worksheet in the workbook.

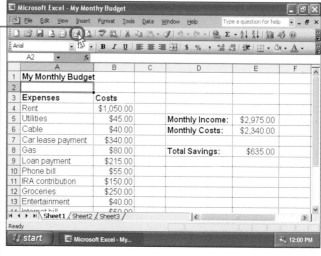

■ If you selected **Page(s)** in step **5**, type the number of the first page you want to print. Press the Tab key and then type the number of the last page you want to print.

**6** Click **OK**.

**QUICKLY PRINT DISPLAYED WORKSHEET**

**1** Click 🖨 to quickly print the worksheet displayed on your screen.

Note: If 🖨 is not displayed, click 📊 on the Standard toolbar to display the button.

# SET A PRINT AREA

If you always print the same area of your worksheet, you can set a print area to quickly print the data. Excel will print only the data in the print area.

If you have not set a print area for your worksheet, Excel will print the entire worksheet.

## SET A PRINT AREA

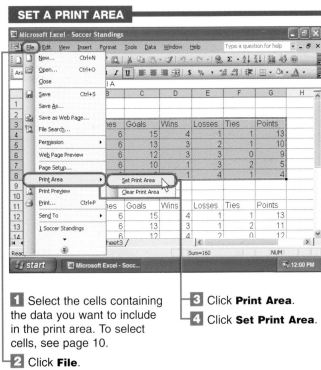

**1** Select the cells containing the data you want to include in the print area. To select cells, see page 10.

**2** Click **File**.

**3** Click **Print Area**.

**4** Click **Set Print Area**.

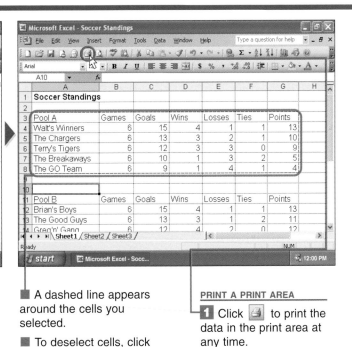

■ A dashed line appears around the cells you selected.

■ To deselect cells, click any cell.

### PRINT A PRINT AREA

**1** Click 🖨 to print the data in the print area at any time.

**Can I include multiple groups of cells in a print area?**

Yes. Including multiple groups of cells in a print area is useful when you want to print data from several sections of a large worksheet. When you set a print area that includes multiple groups of cells, Excel prints each group of cells on a different page. To select multiple groups of cells, see page 10.

**How do I print other data in my worksheet after I set a print area?**

You can temporarily override a print area you have set and print other data in your worksheet. Select the cells containing the data you want to print and then perform steps **2** to **6** starting on page 148, choosing **Selection** in step **4** ( ○ changes to ⊙ ).

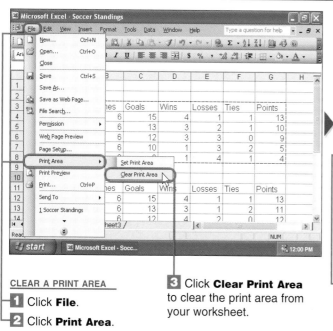

**CLEAR A PRINT AREA**

**1** Click **File**.

**2** Click **Print Area**.

**3** Click **Clear Print Area** to clear the print area from your worksheet.

■ The dashed line disappears from your worksheet.

# CENTER DATA ON A PRINTED PAGE

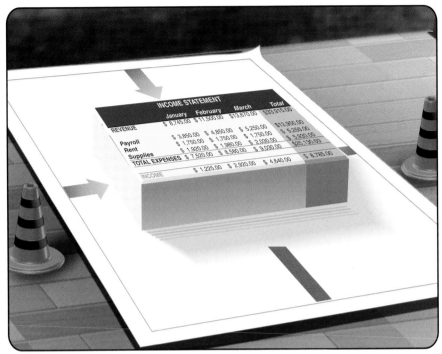

You can center data horizontally and vertically on a printed page.

Centering data on a printed page will not affect the way your worksheet appears on your screen.

CENTER DATA ON A PRINTED PAGE

**1** Click **File**.

**2** Click **Page Setup**.

■ The Page Setup dialog box appears.

**3** Click the **Margins** tab.

**4** Click the way you want to center the data (☐ changes to ☑). You can select both options to horizontally and vertically center the data.

**5** Click **OK** to confirm your change.

*Note: You can use the Print Preview feature to see how your worksheet will appear on a printed page. For information on using the Print Preview feature, see page 146.*

# CHANGE PAGE ORIENTATION

You can change the page orientation to change the way your worksheet appears on a printed page.

Excel automatically prints your worksheets in the portrait orientation. The landscape orientation is useful when you want a wide worksheet to fit on one printed page.

Changing the page orientation will not affect the way your worksheet appears on your screen.

## CHANGE PAGE ORIENTATION

**1** Click **File**.

**2** Click **Page Setup**.

■ The Page Setup dialog box appears.

**3** Click the **Page** tab.

**4** Click the page orientation you want to use (○ changes to ◉).

**5** Click **OK** to confirm your change.

Note: You can use the Print Preview feature to see how your worksheet will appear on a printed page. For information on using the Print Preview feature, see page 146.

# CHANGE MARGINS

You can change the margins in your worksheet. A margin is the amount of space between the data on a page and the edge of your paper.

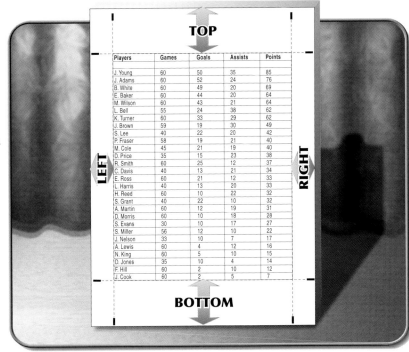

**TOP**

**LEFT**

**RIGHT**

**BOTTOM**

Changing the margins allows you to adjust the amount of information that can fit on a page. You may want to change the margins to accommodate letterhead or other specialty paper.

Changing the margins will not affect the way your worksheet appears on your screen.

## CHANGE MARGINS

**1** Click **File**.

**2** Click **Page Setup**.

■ The Page Setup dialog box appears.

**3** Click the **Margins** tab.

■ These areas display the current margins for your worksheet.

*Note: By default, Excel sets the top and bottom margins to 1 inch and the left and right margins to 0.75 inches.*

**Tip**

**Is there another way to change the margins in my worksheet?**

Yes. You can use the Print Preview feature to change the margins in your worksheet.

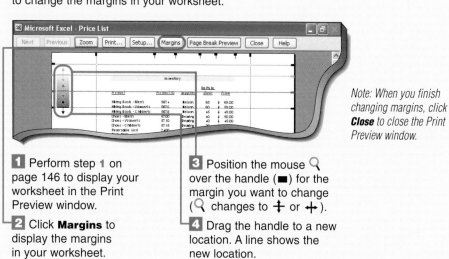

*Note: When you finish changing margins, click* ***Close*** *to close the Print Preview window.*

**1** Perform step **1** on page 146 to display your worksheet in the Print Preview window.

**2** Click **Margins** to display the margins in your worksheet.

**3** Position the mouse ⌕ over the handle (■) for the margin you want to change (⌕ changes to ↕ or ↔).

**4** Drag the handle to a new location. A line shows the new location.

**4** To change a margin, double-click in the box for the margin you want to change.

**5** Type a new margin in inches.

**6** Repeat steps **4** and **5** for each margin you want to change.

**7** Click **OK** to confirm your changes.

*Note: You can use the Print Preview feature to see how your worksheet will appear on a printed page. For information on using the Print Preview feature, see page 146.*

# CHANGE PRINT OPTIONS

You can use the print options that Excel offers to change the way your worksheet appears on a printed page.

Changing the print options will not affect the way your worksheet appears on your screen.

## CHANGE PRINT OPTIONS

**1** Click **File**.

**2** Click **Page Setup**.

■ The Page Setup dialog box appears.

**3** Click the **Sheet** tab.

**4** Click each print option you want to use (☐ changes to ☑ ).

## Tip

### What are some of the print options Excel offers?

**Gridlines**

Prints lines around the cells in your worksheet.

**Black and white**

Prints a colored worksheet in black and white. This is useful when you want to print a colored worksheet on a black-and-white printer.

**Draft quality**

Reduces printing time by not printing gridlines and most graphics.

**Row and column headings**

Prints the row numbers and column letters.

**Cell errors**

Specifies the way cell errors appear on a printed page. For information on cell errors, see page 98.

**5** If you added comments to your worksheet, click this area to print the comments when you print your worksheet.

*Note: For information on comments, see page 58.*

**6** Click an option to specify where you want to print the comments.

**At end of sheet**
Prints comments on a separate page.

**As displayed on sheet**
Prints comments on the worksheet.

■ By default, Excel will print any cell errors that appear in your worksheet.

**7** To specify how you want cell errors to appear when you print your worksheet, click this area.

**8** Click the way you want cell errors to appear.

**9** Click **OK** to confirm your changes.

*Note: You can use the Print Preview feature to see how your worksheet will appear on a printed page. For information on using the Print Preview feature, see page 146.*

# INSERT A PAGE BREAK

You can insert a page break to start a new page at a specific location in your worksheet. A page break indicates where one page ends and another begins.

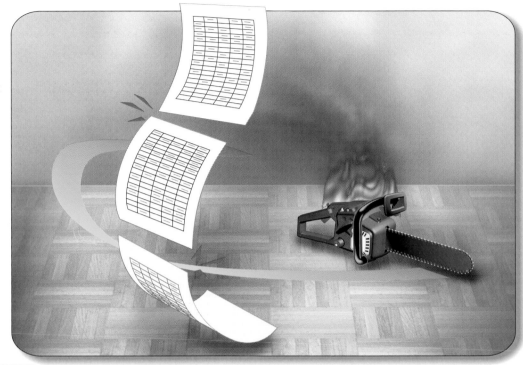

## INSERT A PAGE BREAK

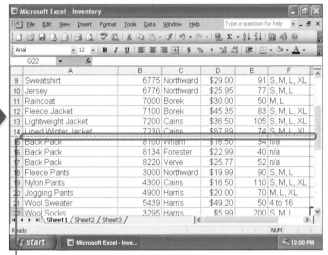

**1** To select the row or column you want to appear at the beginning of the new page, click the heading of the row or column.

**2** Click **Insert**.

**3** Click **Page Break**.

*Note: If Page Break does not appear on the menu, position the mouse over the bottom of the menu to display the menu option.*

■ A dashed line appears on your screen. This line indicates where one page ends and another begins.

■ The dashed line will not appear when you print your worksheet.

■ To deselect a row or column, click any cell.

**Tip**

## Will Excel ever insert page breaks automatically?

When you fill a page with data, Excel automatically inserts a page break to start a new page.

**Tip**

## How do I delete a page break I inserted into my worksheet?

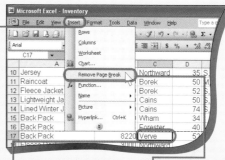

**1** Click a cell directly below or directly to the right of the page break line you want to delete.

**2** Click **Insert**.

**3** Click **Remove Page Break** to delete the page break.

*Note: If Remove Page Break does not appear on the menu, position the mouse ☐ over the bottom of the menu to display the menu option.*

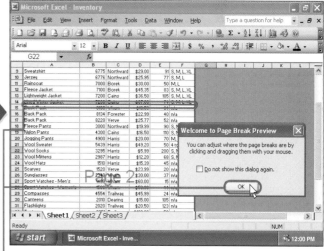

**VIEW ALL PAGE BREAKS**

**1** Click **View**.

**2** Click **Page Break Preview** to display all the page breaks in your worksheet.

■ A dialog box appears.

**3** Click **OK** to close the dialog box.

■ A solid blue line shows the location of a page break you inserted into your worksheet.

*Note: A dashed blue line shows the location of a page break Excel inserted for you.*

■ To return to the normal view at any time, repeat steps **1** and **2**, selecting **Normal** in step **2**.

# ADD A HEADER OR FOOTER

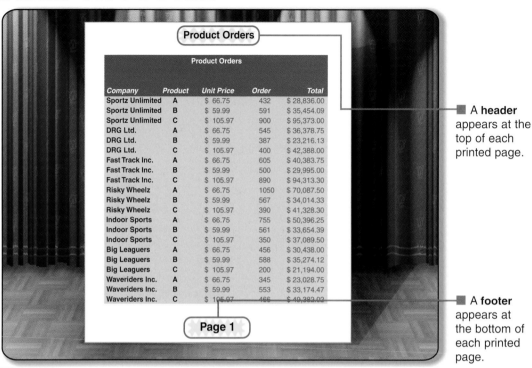

Product Orders

You can add a header or footer to display additional information on each page of your worksheet. A header or footer can contain information such as your name, the page number and the current date.

■ A **header** appears at the top of each printed page.

■ A **footer** appears at the bottom of each printed page.

Page 1

---

ADD A HEADER OR FOOTER

**1** Click **View**.

**2** Click **Header and Footer**.

*Note: If Header and Footer does not appear on the menu, position the mouse ⩲ over the bottom of the menu to display the menu option.*

■ The Page Setup dialog box appears.

**3** To view a list of available headers, click this area.

**4** Click the header you want to use.

**Tip**

**Can I see how a header or footer will look before I print my worksheet?**

Yes. You can use the Print Preview feature to see how a header or footer will look before you print your worksheet. For information on using the Print Preview feature, see page 146.

■ This area displays how the header will appear at the top of a page.

**5** To view a list of available footers, click this area.

**6** Click the footer you want to use.

■ This area displays how the footer will appear at the bottom of a page.

**7** Click **OK** to add the header or footer to your worksheet.

■ To remove a header or footer from your worksheet, repeat steps **1** to **7**, selecting **(none)** in step **4** or step **6**.

# ADD A CUSTOM HEADER OR FOOTER

You can add a custom header or footer to every page of your worksheet. Adding a custom header or footer allows you to specify the information the header or footer displays.

A custom header or footer can contain information such as your e-mail address.

## ADD A CUSTOM HEADER OR FOOTER

**1** Click **View**.

**2** Click **Header and Footer**.

*Note: If Header and Footer does not appear on the menu, position the mouse ⌖ over the bottom of the menu to display the menu option.*

■ The Page Setup dialog box appears.

**3** Click the appropriate button to create a custom header or footer.

■ A dialog box appears, displaying areas for the left, center and right sections of the page.

**Tip**

### How can Excel help me create a custom header or footer?

You can click one of the following buttons to enter or format information in a custom header or footer.

| | | | |
|---|---|---|---|
| A | Format header or footer text | | Insert workbook path and name |
| | Insert page number | | Insert workbook name |
| | Insert total number of pages | | Insert worksheet name |
| | Insert current date | | Insert picture |
| | Insert current time | | Format picture |

**4** Click the area for the section of the page where you want to display a custom header or footer.

*Note: If text appears in the area, drag the mouse I over the text until you highlight the text. Then press the Delete key to remove the text.*

**5** Type the header or footer text.

**6** Click **OK** to confirm your changes.

■ These areas display how the custom header or footer will appear on a printed page.

**7** Click **OK** to add the custom header or footer to your worksheet.

*Note: You can use the Print Preview feature to see how your worksheet will appear on a printed page. For information on using the Print Preview feature, see page 146.*

# CHANGE SIZE OF PRINTED DATA

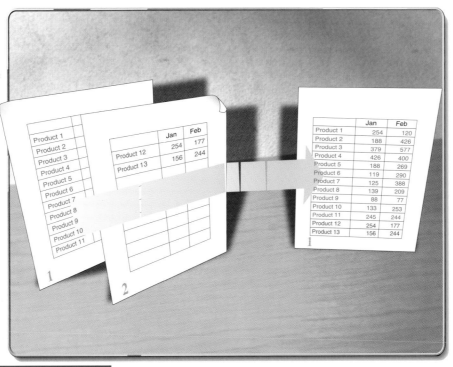

You can reduce the size of printed data to print your worksheet on a specific number of pages.

Changing the size of printed data is useful when the last page of your worksheet contains a small amount of data that you want to fit on the previous page.

CHANGE SIZE OF PRINTED DATA

**1** Click **File**.

**2** Click **Page Setup**.

■ The Page Setup dialog box appears.

**3** Click the **Page** tab.

**4** Click **Fit to** to fit the worksheet on a specific number of pages (○ changes to ◉).

**Tip**

**What should I consider when changing the size of printed data?**

When specifying the number of pages you want to print data across and down, you must consider the amount of data you need to print. If you try to fit the data on too few pages, the data may become too small to read.

**Tip**

**Why did the page breaks in my worksheet disappear when I changed the size of printed data?**

When you change the size of printed data, Excel ignores any page breaks you have inserted into your worksheet. This allows Excel to fit the worksheet data on the number of pages you specify. For information on inserting page breaks, see page 158.

**5** Type the number of pages you want the data to print across.

**6** Press the Tab key and then type the number of pages you want the data to print down.

**7** Click **OK** to confirm your changes.

■ Excel will change the size of the printed data to fit on the number of pages you specified.

*Note: You can use the Print Preview feature to see how your worksheet will appear on a printed page. For information on the Print Preview feature, see page 146.*

# REPEAT LABELS ON PRINTED PAGES

You can display the same row or column labels on every printed page of a worksheet. This can help you review worksheets that print on several pages.

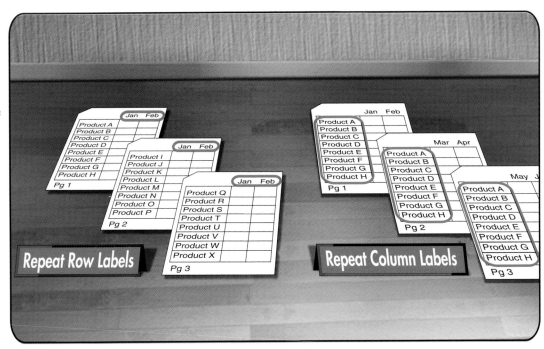

Repeat Row Labels

Repeat Column Labels

## REPEAT LABELS ON PRINTED PAGES

**1** Click **File**.

**2** Click **Page Setup**.

■ The Page Setup dialog box appears.

**3** Click the **Sheet** tab.

**4** Click 📇 beside one of the following options.

**Rows to repeat at top**

Repeat labels across the top of each page.

**Columns to repeat at left**

Repeat labels down the left side of each page.

**Tip**

**Can I see how the repeated labels will look before I print my worksheet?**

You can use the Print Preview feature to see how the repeated labels will look before you print your worksheet. For information on using the Print Preview feature, see page 146.

**Tip**

**How do I stop repeating labels on printed pages?**

Perform steps **1** to **3** below. Then drag the mouse I over the text in the area beside the appropriate option until you highlight the text. Press the Delete key to remove the text from the area and then perform step **7**.

■ The Page Setup dialog box collapses to one line so you can clearly view the data in your worksheet.

**5** Click a cell in the row or column containing the labels you want to repeat.

■ A moving outline appears around the row or column.

**6** Click 🖳 to redisplay the entire Page Setup dialog box.

■ The information for the row or column you selected appears.

**7** Click **OK** to confirm your changes.

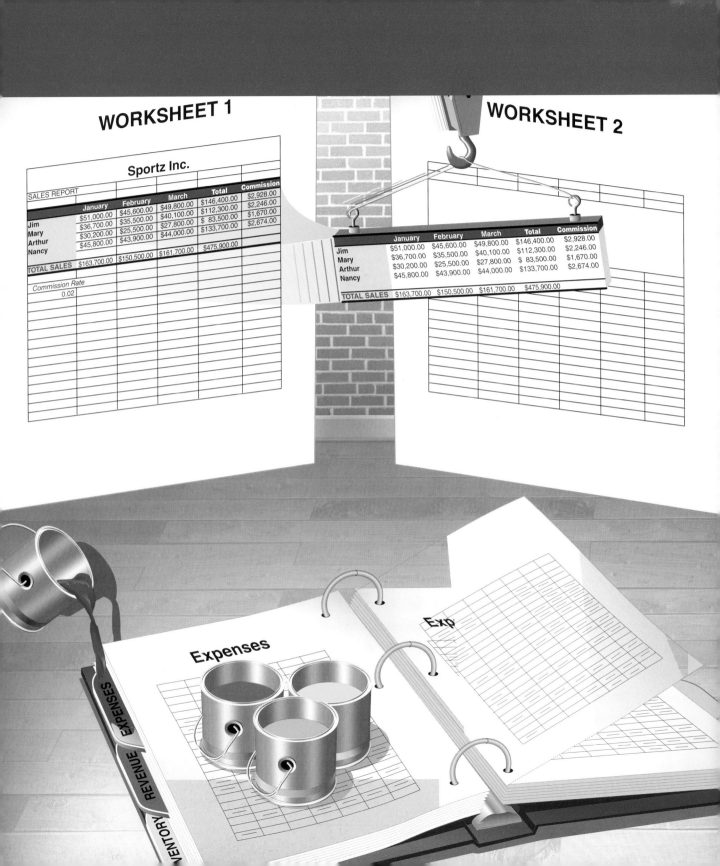

## CHAPTER 9

# Work With Multiple Worksheets

*Do you want to work with more than one worksheet at a time? This chapter teaches you how to switch between worksheets, move or copy data between worksheets, color worksheet tabs and more.*

# SWITCH BETWEEN WORKSHEETS

A workbook contains several worksheets. You can easily switch between the worksheets in your workbook to view and compare all the data.

Worksheets can help you organize information in your workbook. For example, you can store information for each division of a company on a separate worksheet.

## SWITCH BETWEEN WORKSHEETS

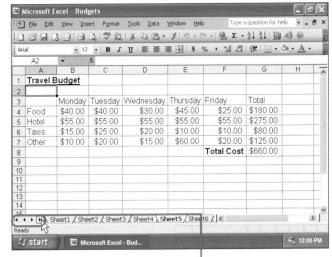

■ This area displays a tab for each worksheet in your workbook. The displayed worksheet has a white tab.

**1** Click the tab for the worksheet you want to display.

■ The worksheet you selected appears.
The contents of the other worksheets in your workbook are hidden behind the displayed worksheet.

**BROWSE THROUGH WORKSHEET TABS**

■ If you have many worksheets in your workbook, you may not be able to see all the worksheet tabs.

*Note: To insert additional worksheets, see page 172.*

**1** Click one of the following buttons to browse through the worksheet tabs.

⏮ Display first tab

◀ Display previous tab

▶ Display next tab

⏭ Display last tab

# RENAME A WORKSHEET

You can rename a worksheet in your workbook to better describe the contents of the worksheet.

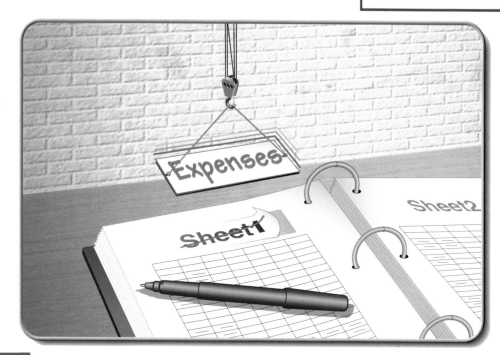

Each worksheet in a workbook must have a unique name. Short worksheet names are generally better than long names since short names allow you to display more worksheet tabs on your screen at once.

## RENAME A WORKSHEET

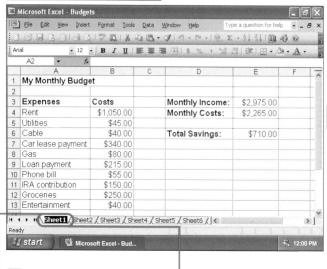

**1** Double-click the tab for the worksheet you want to rename.

■ The name of the worksheet is highlighted.

**2** Type a new name for the worksheet and then press the Enter key.

*Note: A worksheet name can contain up to 31 characters, including spaces.*

# INSERT A WORKSHEET

You can insert a new worksheet anywhere in your workbook to include additional information.

Each workbook you create automatically contains three worksheets. You can insert as many new worksheets as you need.

## INSERT A WORKSHEET

**1** Click the tab for the worksheet you want to appear after the new worksheet.

**2** Click **Insert**.

**3** Click **Worksheet**.

■ The new worksheet appears.

■ Excel displays a tab for the new worksheet.

You can permanently remove a worksheet you no longer need from your workbook.

You cannot restore a worksheet once it has been deleted from your workbook.

## DELETE A WORKSHEET

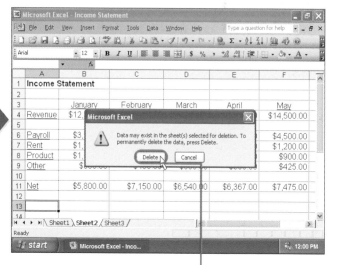

**1** Click the tab for the worksheet you want to delete.

**2** Click **Edit**.

**3** Click **Delete Sheet**.

*Note: If Delete Sheet does not appear on the menu, position the mouse ▷ over the bottom of the menu to display the menu option.*

■ A warning dialog box may appear, stating that Excel will permanently delete the data in the worksheet.

**4** Click **Delete** to permanently delete the worksheet.

# MOVE A WORKSHEET

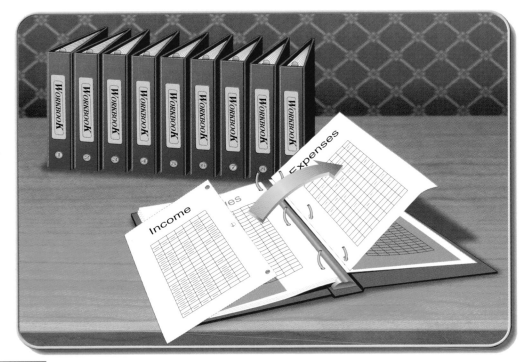

You can move a worksheet to a new location in your workbook. This allows you to reorganize the data in your workbook.

## MOVE A WORKSHEET

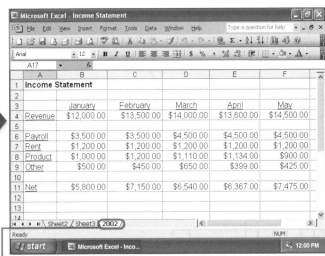

**1** Position the mouse ⌖ over the tab for the worksheet you want to move.

**2** Drag the worksheet to a new location.

■ An arrow ( ▼ ) shows where the worksheet will appear.

■ The worksheet appears in the new location.

# ADD COLOR TO A WORKSHEET TAB

You can add color to a worksheet tab to make the tab stand out. This allows you to quickly locate a worksheet of interest.

Adding color to worksheet tabs can also help you organize a workbook that contains several worksheets. For example, you can add the same color to the tabs of worksheets that contain similar data.

## ADD COLOR TO A WORKSHEET TAB

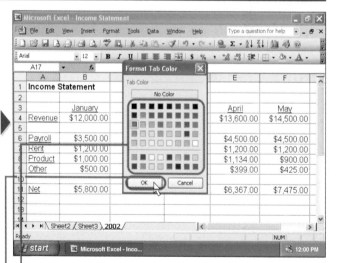

**1** Click the worksheet tab you want to add color to.

**2** Click **Format**.

**3** Click **Sheet**.

**4** Click **Tab Color**.

■ The Format Tab Color dialog box appears.

**5** Click the color you want to use.

**6** Click **OK**.

■ Excel adds the color you selected to the worksheet tab.

■ To remove color from a worksheet tab, repeat steps **1** to **6**, selecting **No Color** in step **5**.

# MOVE OR COPY DATA BETWEEN WORKSHEETS

You can move or copy data from one worksheet to another. This will save you time when you want to use data from another worksheet.

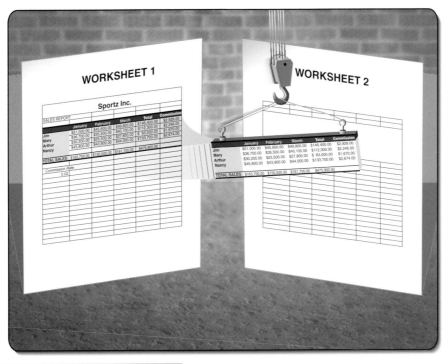

WORKSHEET 1

WORKSHEET 2

Sportz Inc.

When you move data, the data disappears from its original location.

When you copy data, the data appears in both the original and new locations.

## MOVE OR COPY DATA BETWEEN WORKSHEETS

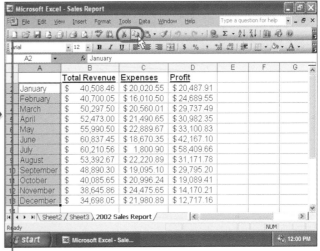

**1** Select the cells containing the data you want to move or copy to another worksheet. To select cells, see page 10.

**2** Click one of the following buttons.

✂ Move data

📋 Copy data

■ The Clipboard task pane may appear, displaying items you have selected to move or copy. To use the Clipboard task pane, see the top of page 177.

**Tip**

**How can I use the Clipboard task pane to move or copy data?**

The Clipboard task pane displays up to the last 24 items you have selected to move or copy. To place a clipboard item into your worksheet, click the cell where you want to place the item and then click the item in the task pane. For more information on the task pane, see page 16.

**Tip**

**Why does the Paste Options button (📋) appear after I copy data?**

You can use the Paste Options button (📋) to change the way Excel copies data. For example, you can specify that you want to use the column width from the original cells in the new location. Click the Paste Options button to display a list of options and then select the option you want to use. The Paste Options button disappears after you perform another task.

**3** Click the tab for the worksheet where you want to place the data.

*Note: To place the data in another workbook, open the workbook before performing step 3. To open a workbook, see page 32.*

**4** Click the cell where you want to place the data. This cell will become the top left cell of the new location.

**5** Click 📋 to place the data in the new location.

■ The data appears in the new location.

*Note: If number signs (#) appear in a cell, the column is too narrow to fit the data. To change the column width, see page 66.*

# ENTER A FORMULA ACROSS WORKSHEETS

You can enter a formula that uses data from more than one worksheet.

If you change a number used in a formula you entered across worksheets, Excel will automatically redo the calculation for you. This ensures your calculations are always up to date.

## ENTER A FORMULA ACROSS WORKSHEETS

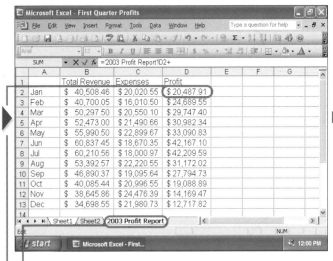

**1** Click the cell where you want to enter a formula.

**2** Type an equal sign (=) to begin the formula.

**3** Click the tab for the worksheet containing the data you want to use in the formula.

**4** Click a cell containing data you want to use in the formula.

**5** Type the operator for the calculation you want to perform. For information on the types of operators you can use, see the top of page 179.

**Tip**

**When entering a formula, what types of operators can I use?**

**Arithmetic operators** allow you to perform mathematical calculations.

| Arithmetic Operator: | Description: |
|---|---|
| + | Addition (A1+B1) |
| - | Subtraction (A1-B1) |
| * | Multiplication (A1*B1) |
| / | Division (A1/B1) |
| % | Percent (A1%) |
| ^ | Exponentiation (A1^B1) |

**Comparison operators** allow you to compare two values. A formula that uses only a comparison operator will return a value of TRUE or FALSE.

| Comparison Operator: | Description: |
|---|---|
| = | Equal to (A1=B1) |
| > | Greater than (A1>B1) |
| < | Less than (A1<B1) |
| >= | Greater than or equal to (A1>=B1) |
| <= | Less than or equal to (A1<=B1) |
| <> | Not equal to (A1<>B1) |

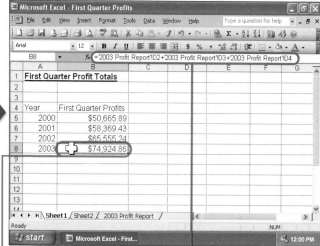

**6** Repeat steps **3** to **5** until you have selected all the cells containing the data you want to use in the formula.

*Note: In this example, cells **D2** to **D4** are added together.*

**7** Press the **Enter** key to complete the formula.

■ The result of the calculation appears in the cell you selected in step **1**.

**8** To view the formula you entered, click the cell containing the formula.

■ The formula bar displays the worksheet name and cell reference for each cell used in the formula.

# USING THE WATCH WINDOW TOOLBAR

You can use the Watch Window toolbar to see the results of formulas on other worksheets. This saves you from having to switch between worksheets to keep track of formulas of interest.

Using the Watch Window toolbar is useful when you want to watch a formula you entered across worksheets. To enter a formula across worksheets, see page 178.

## USING THE WATCH WINDOW TOOLBAR

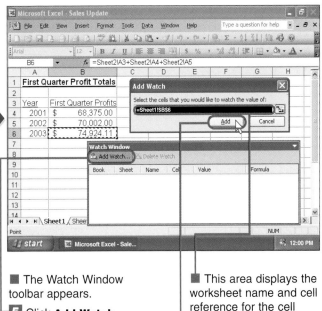

**1** Click a cell containing a formula you want to watch.

**2** Click **Tools**.

**3** Click **Formula Auditing**.

**4** Click **Show Watch Window**.

*Note: If Show Watch Window does not appear on the menu, position the mouse ℜ over the bottom of the menu to display the menu option.*

■ The Watch Window toolbar appears.

**5** Click **Add Watch** to add the formula you selected in step **1** to the Watch Window toolbar.

■ The Add Watch dialog box appears.

■ This area displays the worksheet name and cell reference for the cell containing the formula.

**6** Click **Add** to add the formula to the Watch Window toolbar.

**Tip**

**How do I change the width of a column in the Watch Window toolbar?**

**1** To change the width of a column, position the mouse ⌖ over the right edge of the column heading (⌖ changes to ✛).

**2** Drag the column edge until the column displays the width you want.

**Tip**

**What information appears in the Watch Window toolbar?**

■ The name of the workbook containing the formula.

■ The name of the worksheet containing the formula.

■ The name of the cell containing the formula. To name cells, see page 56.

■ The cell reference of the cell containing the formula.

■ The result of the formula.

■ The formula you are watching.

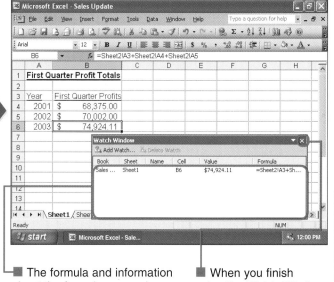

■ The formula and information about the formula appear in the Watch Window toolbar.

■ When you change data used in the formula, the Watch Window toolbar will display the new result of the formula.

■ When you finish using the Watch Window toolbar, click ✕ to hide the toolbar.

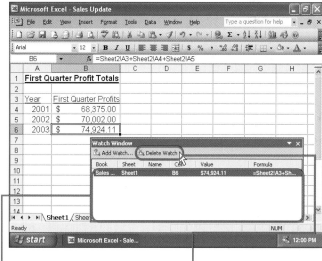

**STOP WATCHING A FORMULA**

**1** Click the formula you want to stop watching.

**2** Click **Delete Watch**.

■ The formula disappears from the Watch Window toolbar.

181

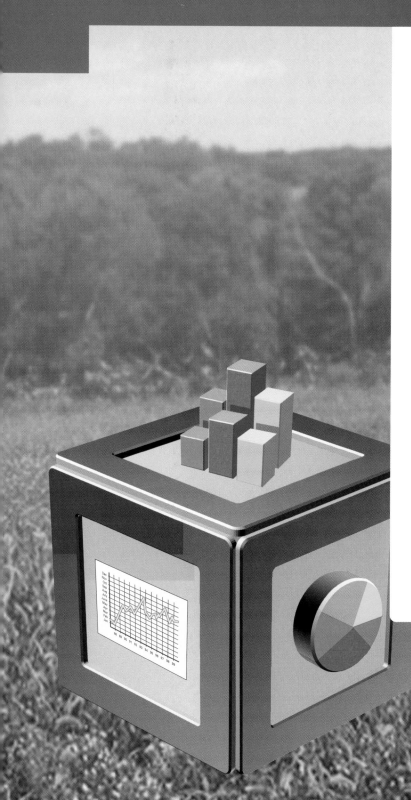

## CHAPTER 10

# Work With Charts

Are you interested in displaying your worksheet data in a chart? In this chapter, you will learn how to create, change and print charts.

# INTRODUCTION TO CHARTS

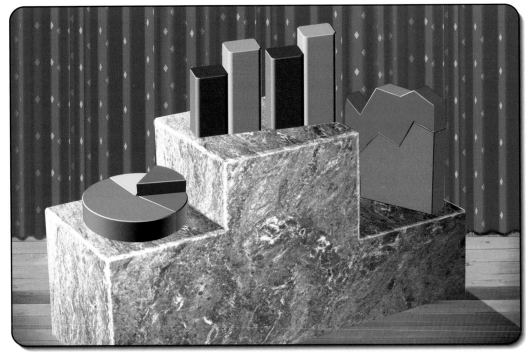

A chart allows you to visually display your worksheet data and can help you compare data and view trends. Excel offers many different chart types.

## PARTS OF A CHART

### Data Series

A group of related data representing one row or column from your worksheet. Each data series is represented by a specific color, pattern or symbol.

### Chart Title

Identifies the subject of your chart.

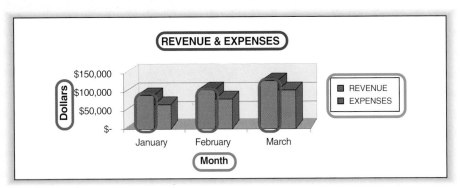

### Legend

Identifies the color, pattern or symbol that represents each data series in your chart.

### Value Axis Title

Indicates the unit of measure used in your chart.

### Category Axis Title

Indicates the categories used in your chart.

## COMMON CHART TYPES

### Area

An area chart is useful for showing the amount of change in data over time. Each area represents a data series.

### Line

A line chart is useful for showing changes to data at regular intervals. Each line represents a data series.

### Column

A column chart is useful for showing changes to data over time or comparing individual items. Each column represents an item in a data series.

### Bar

A bar chart is useful for comparing individual items. Each bar represents an item in a data series.

### Pie

A pie chart is useful for showing the relationship of parts to a whole. Each piece of a pie represents an item in a data series. A pie chart can show only one data series at a time.

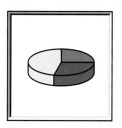

### Doughnut

A doughnut chart is useful for showing the relationship of parts to a whole. Unlike a pie chart, a doughnut chart can display more than one data series. Each ring represents a data series.

### Radar

A radar chart is useful for comparing the items in several data series. Each data series is shown as a line around a central point.

### XY (Scatter)

An XY (scatter) chart is useful for showing the relationship between two or more data series measured at uneven intervals.

# CREATE A CHART

You can create a chart to graphically display your worksheet data. Charts allow you to easily compare data and view patterns and trends.

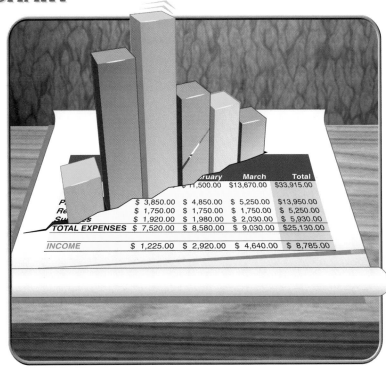

The Chart Wizard takes you step by step through the process of creating a chart.

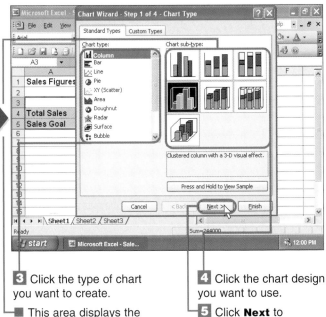

**1** Select the cells containing the data you want to display in a chart, including the row and column labels. To select cells, see page 10.

**2** Click 📊 to create a chart.

*Note: If 📊 is not displayed, click 📊 on the Standard toolbar to display the button.*

■ The Chart Wizard appears.

**3** Click the type of chart you want to create.

■ This area displays the available chart designs for the type of chart you selected.

**4** Click the chart design you want to use.

**5** Click **Next** to continue.

**Tip**

**Can I see a preview of my chart when I'm choosing the chart type and design?**

Yes. After performing step **4** below, you can press and hold down the **Press and Hold to View Sample** button to see a preview of how your chart will appear with the chart type and design you selected.

**Tip**

**What titles can I add to my chart?**

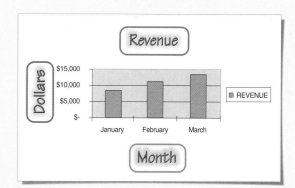

**Chart title**
Identifies the subject of your chart.

**Value axis**
Indicates the unit of measure used in your chart.

**Category axis**
Indicates the categories used in your chart.

**6** Click an option to specify the way you want Excel to plot the data from your worksheet ( ○ changes to ⊙ ).

■ This area displays a preview of the chart.

**7** Click **Next** to continue.

■ You can click **Back** at any time to return to a previous step and change your selections.

■ This area provides boxes you can use to add titles to the chart.

*Note: Some boxes are not available for some chart types.*

**8** To add a title to the chart, click a box and type the title. Repeat this step for each title you want to add.

■ This area shows how the titles will appear in the chart.

**9** Click **Next** to continue.

**CONTINUED**

# CREATE A CHART

When creating a chart, you can choose to display the chart on the same worksheet as the data or on its own sheet, called a chart sheet.

Displaying a chart with your worksheet data is useful when you want to print the chart and data on the same page.

Displaying a chart on a chart sheet is useful when you want to view a chart separately from your worksheet data.

## CREATE A CHART (CONTINUED)

**10** Click an option to specify where you want to display the chart (○ changes to ◉).

**As new sheet** - Displays the chart on its own sheet, called a chart sheet.

**As object in** - Displays the chart on the same worksheet as the data.

■ If you selected **As new sheet** in step **10**, you can type a name for the chart sheet in this area.

**11** Click **Finish** to create the chart.

**Tip**

**What happens if I change the data I used to create a chart?**

If you change the data you used to create a chart, Excel will automatically update the chart to display the changes.

**Tip**

**Is there a way to quickly create a chart?**

Yes. To quickly create a basic chart, select the cells containing the data you want to display in the chart and then press the F11 key. The chart will appear on its own chart sheet.

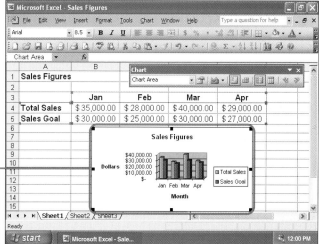

■ In this example, the chart appears on the same worksheet as the data.

■ The Chart toolbar also appears, displaying buttons that allow you to make changes to the chart.

■ Excel outlines the data you selected to create the chart.

■ The handles (■) around a chart let you change the size of the chart. To hide the handles, click outside the chart.

*Note: To move or resize a chart, see page 190.*

**DELETE A CHART**

**1** Click a blank area in the chart you want to delete. Handles (■) appear around the chart.

**2** Press the Delete key to delete the chart.

*Note: To delete a chart displayed on a chart sheet, you must delete the sheet. To delete a worksheet, see page 173.*

# MOVE OR RESIZE A CHART

You can change the location and size of a chart displayed on your worksheet.

Moving a chart to another location in your worksheet is useful if the chart covers your data. Increasing the size of a chart is useful if the information in the chart is too small to read.

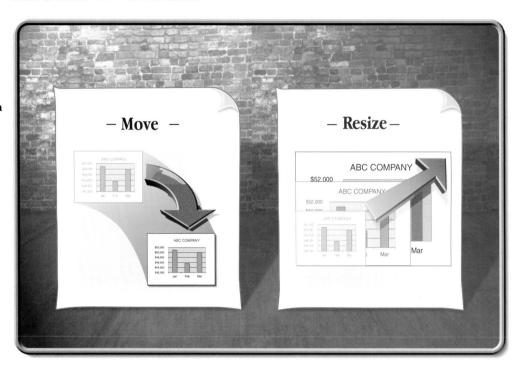

— Move —

— Resize —

## MOVE A CHART

**1** Position the mouse ⊕ over a blank area in the chart you want to move (⊕ changes to ⬉).

**2** Drag the chart to a new location in your worksheet.

■ A dashed line indicates where the chart will appear.

■ The chart appears in the new location.

■ To deselect the chart, click outside the chart.

**Tip**

**What handle (■) should I use to resize a chart?**

■ Changes the height of a chart

■ Changes the width of a chart

■ Changes the height and width of a chart at the same time

**Tip**

**Can I move individual items in a chart?**

Yes. To move the chart title, an axis title or the legend to a new location in a chart, position the mouse ⟍ over the item. Then drag the item to a new location. You cannot move an item outside of the chart area.

## RESIZE A CHART

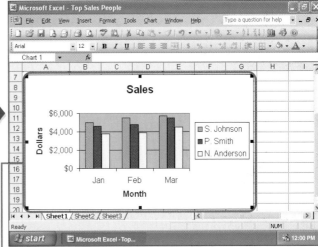

**1** Click a blank area in the chart you want to resize. Handles (■) appear around the chart.

**2** Position the mouse ⟍ over one of the handles (⟍ changes to ⤡, ⤢, ↔ or ↕).

**3** Drag the handle until the chart is the size you want.

■ A dashed line shows the new size.

■ The chart appears in the new size.

■ To deselect the chart, click outside the chart.

# PRINT A CHART

You can print
your chart with
the worksheet
data or on its
own page.

Print a chart with
worksheet data

Print a chart on
its own page

When you print a
chart on its own
page, the chart
will expand to fill
the page.

## PRINT A CHART

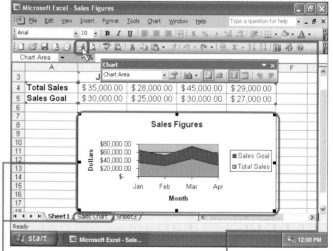

**PRINT A CHART WITH
WORKSHEET DATA**

■1 Click a cell outside
the chart.

■2 Click 🖨 to print
the chart with your
worksheet data.

*Note: If 🖨 is not displayed,
click ╪ on the Standard
toolbar to display the button.*

**PRINT A CHART ON ITS OWN PAGE**

■1 To print a chart displayed
on a worksheet, click a blank
area in the chart.

■ To print a chart displayed
on a chart sheet, click the tab
for the chart sheet.

■2 Click 🖨 to print
the chart on its own
page.

*Note: If 🖨 is not
displayed, click ╪ on
the Standard toolbar to
display the button.*

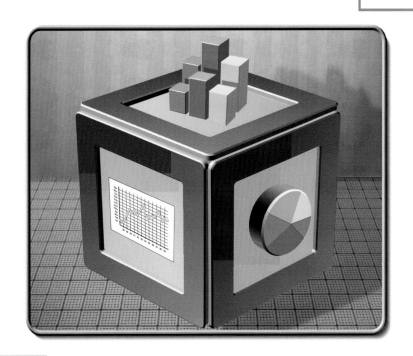

**After you create a
chart, you can
change the chart
type to present
your data more
effectively.**

The type of chart you
should use depends on
your data. For example,
area, column and line
charts are ideal for
showing changes to
values over time. Pie
charts are ideal for
showing percentages.

## CHANGE THE CHART TYPE

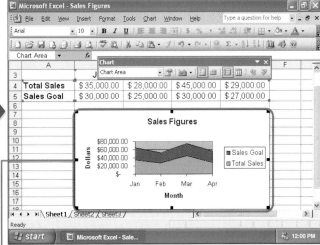

**1** Click a blank area in the
chart you want to change.
Handles (■) appear
around the chart.

**2** Click ⏷ in this area to
display the available chart
types.

*Note: If the Chart toolbar is
not displayed, see page 111
to display the toolbar.*

**3** Click the type of
chart you want to use.

■ The chart displays the
chart type you selected.

■ To deselect the chart,
click outside the chart.

# CHANGE CHART TITLES

You can change the chart and axis titles in a chart to make the titles more meaningful.

## CHANGE CHART TITLES

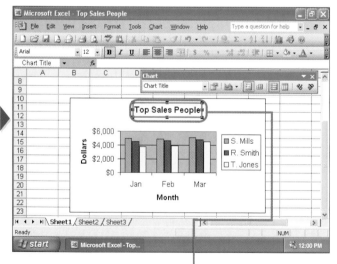

**1** Click the title you want to change. A box appears around the title.

**2** Type the new title.

■ The formula bar displays the title as you type.

**3** Press the Enter key to add the title to the chart.

■ The chart displays the new title.

■ To deselect the title, click outside the chart.

# ROTATE CHART TEXT

You can rotate text on a chart axis to improve the appearance of the chart.

Excel also allows you to rotate the chart and axis titles in a chart.

## ROTATE CHART TEXT

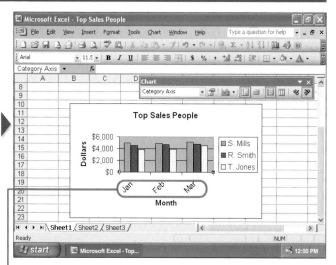

**1** Click the text you want to rotate.

**2** Click one of the following buttons.

⯗ Rotate text downward

⯗ Rotate text upward

*Note: If the Chart toolbar is not displayed, see page 111 to display the toolbar.*

■ Excel rotates the text in the chart.

■ To deselect the text, click outside the chart.

■ To return the text to its original position, repeat steps **1** and **2**.

195

# FORMAT CHART TEXT

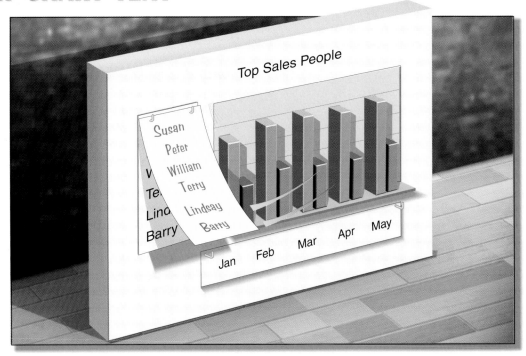

You can enhance the appearance of a chart by changing the font, size or style of text.

## FORMAT CHART TEXT

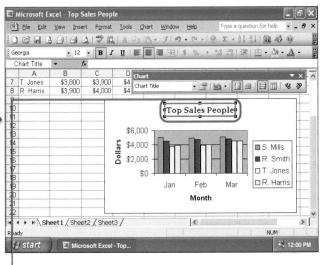

**CHANGE THE FONT**

**1** Click the text you want to change to a different font.

**2** Click ⦁ in this area to display a list of the available fonts.

**3** Click the font you want to use.

■ The text displays the font you selected.

■ To deselect the text, click outside the chart.

196

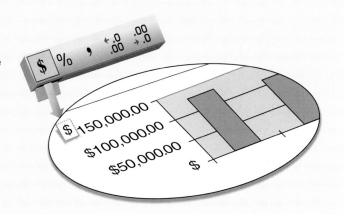

**Tip**

**Can I format numbers in a chart?**

Yes. Click the numbers you want to format and then perform the steps below. You can also click one of the following buttons on the Formatting toolbar to change the style of selected numbers in a chart.

$ Currency

% Percent

, Comma

Add a decimal place

Remove a decimal place

**CHANGE THE SIZE**

**1** Click the text you want to change to a new size.

**2** Click ▾ in this area to display a list of the available sizes.

**3** Click the size you want to use.

**BOLD, ITALICIZE OR UNDERLINE**

**1** Click the text you want to bold, italicize or underline.

**2** Click one of the following buttons.

**B** Bold

*I* Italic

U Underline

■ To remove a bold, italic or underline style, repeat steps **1** and **2**.

# ADD DATA TO A CHART

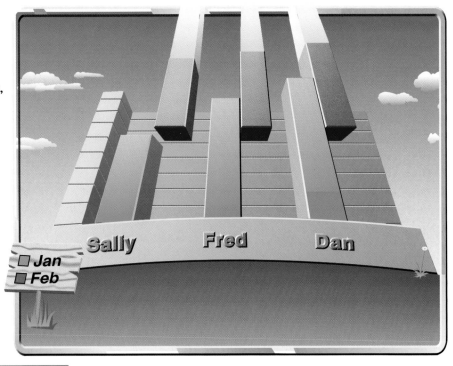

After you create a chart, you can add new data to the chart.

Adding data to a chart is useful when you need to update the chart. For example, you can add the latest sales figures to your chart at the end of each month.

## ADD DATA TO A CHART

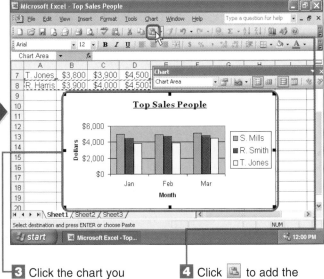

**1** Select the cells containing the data you want to add to the chart, including the row or column labels. To select cells, see page 10.

**2** Click 🖹 to copy the data.

**3** Click the chart you want to add the data to.

**4** Click 🖹 to add the data to the chart.

**Tip**

**Can I add a data series to a pie chart?**

A pie chart can display only one data series. You cannot add another data series to a pie chart.

**Tip**

**How can I add a data series to a chart displayed on a chart sheet?**

To add a data series to a chart displayed on a chart sheet, perform steps **1** and **2** on page 198. Click the tab for the chart sheet containing the chart you want to add the data series to and then perform step **4**.

■ The data appears in the chart.

■ When you add data to a chart, Excel automatically updates the chart legend.

**DELETE DATA FROM A CHART**

**1** Click the data you want to remove from the chart. Handles (■) appear on the data series.

**2** Press the Delete key to delete the data from the chart.

# ADD A DATA TABLE TO A CHART

You can add a
table to a chart
to display the
data used to
create the chart.

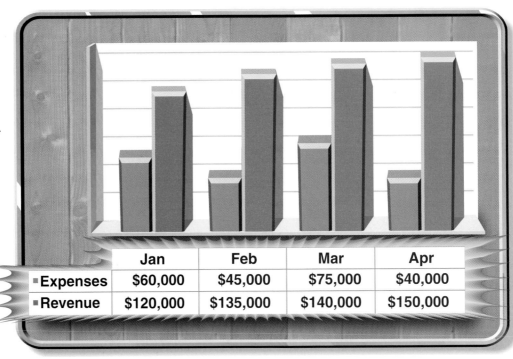

| | Jan | Feb | Mar | Apr |
|---|---|---|---|---|
| ▪Expenses | $60,000 | $45,000 | $75,000 | $40,000 |
| ▪Revenue | $120,000 | $135,000 | $140,000 | $150,000 |

## ADD A DATA TABLE TO A CHART

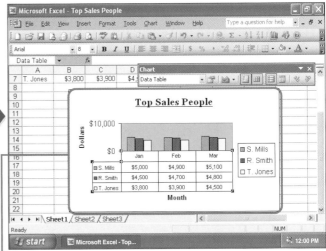

**1** Click a blank area in the
chart you want to change.
Handles (■) appear around
the chart.

*Note: You cannot add a data table
to some types of charts.*

**2** Click 🔲 to add a
data table to the chart.

*Note: If the Chart toolbar is
not displayed, see page 111
to display the toolbar.*

■ The chart displays the
data table.

*Note: If data in the data table is
hidden, you may have to change
the width of the chart. To resize
a chart, see page 190.*

■ To deselect the chart,
click outside the chart.

■ To remove the data
table from the chart,
repeat steps **1** and **2**.

You can change
the way Excel plots
the data in a chart.
This allows you to
emphasize different
information in the
chart.

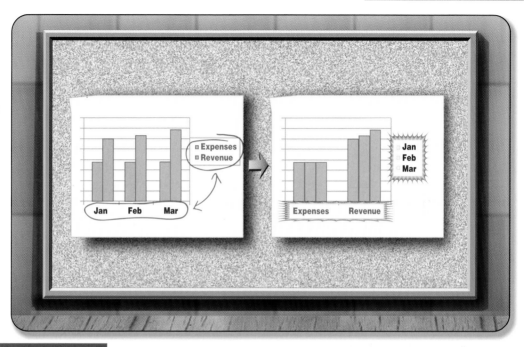

## CHANGE THE WAY DATA IS PLOTTED

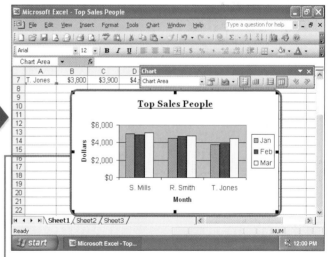

**1** Click a blank area in the
chart you want to change.
Handles (■) appear around
the chart.

**2** Click one of the
following buttons:

🔲 Plot data by row

🔲 Plot data by column

*Note: If the Chart toolbar is
not displayed, see page 111
to display the toolbar.*

■ The chart displays
the change.

■ To deselect the chart,
click outside the chart.

You can change
the color of a data
series in a chart.
You can also add
a pattern to a
data series.

If you will print your
chart on a black-and-
white printer, adding
a pattern to a data
series may make it
easier to identify the
data series in the chart.

When you change
the appearance of
a data series, Excel
automatically updates
the chart legend.

## CHANGE THE COLOR OF A DATA SERIES

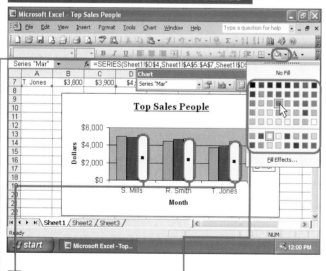

**1** Click the data series you
want to change to a different
color. Handles (■) appear
on the data series.

**2** Click ⋅ in this area to
display the available colors.

**3** Click the color you
want to use.

■ The data series displays
the color you selected.

## ADD A PATTERN TO A DATA SERIES

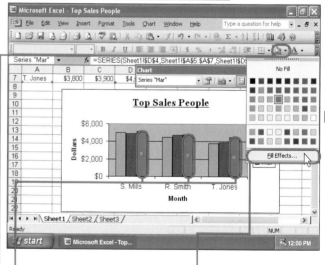

**1** Click the data series
you want to add a pattern to.
Handles (■) appear on the
data series.

**2** Click ⋅ in this area.

**3** Click **Fill Effects**.

■ The Fill Effects dialog
box appears.

### Can I change the appearance of other parts of a chart?

You can change the appearance of other parts of a chart, such as the background of the chart or the chart legend.

To change the color of part of a chart, click the part you want to change. Then perform steps **2** and **3** on page 202 to select the color you want to use.

To add a pattern to part of a chart, click the part you want to change. Then perform steps **2** to **6** starting on page 202 to select the pattern you want to use.

**4** Click the **Pattern** tab.

**5** Click the pattern you want to use.

■ These areas display the foreground and background colors for the current patterns. You can click an area to select a different color.

**6** Click **OK** to confirm your changes.

■ The data series displays the pattern you selected.

■ To deselect the data series, click outside the chart.

## CHAPTER 11

# Work With Objects

*Are you wondering how to use objects, such as AutoShapes and clip art images, to enhance the appearance of your worksheet? This chapter shows you how.*

Hockey Stats

| | Wins | Losses | Ties |
|---|---|---|---|
| | 25 | 21 | 13 |

# ADD WORDART

You can add WordArt to your worksheet or chart to create an eye-catching title or draw attention to important information.

WordArt allows you to create decorative text that is skewed, curved, rotated, stretched, three-dimensional or even vertical.

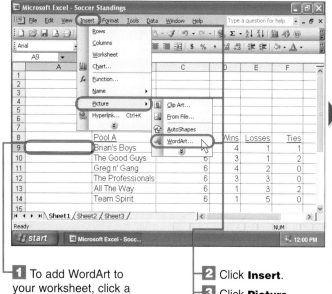

**1** To add WordArt to your worksheet, click a cell in the worksheet.

■ To add WordArt to a chart, click the chart.

**2** Click **Insert**.

**3** Click **Picture**.

**4** Click **WordArt**.

■ The WordArt Gallery dialog box appears.

**5** Click the WordArt style you want to use.

**6** Click **OK** to confirm your selection.

**How do I edit WordArt text?**

To edit WordArt text, double-click the WordArt to display the Edit WordArt Text dialog box. Then perform steps **7** and **8** below to specify the new text you want the WordArt to display.

Click
Click

**Why does the WordArt toolbar appear when I select WordArt in a worksheet or chart?**

The WordArt toolbar contains buttons that allow you to change the appearance of WordArt. For example, you can click one of the following buttons to alter the appearance of WordArt.

Aa Display all the letters in the WordArt at the same height.

Display the WordArt text vertically rather than horizontally.

■ The Edit WordArt Text dialog box appears.

**7** Type the text you want the WordArt to display.

**8** Click **OK** to add the WordArt to your worksheet or chart.

■ The WordArt appears. The handles (O) around the WordArt allow you to change the size of the WordArt. To move or resize WordArt, see page 218.

■ To deselect WordArt, click outside the WordArt.

**DELETE WORDART**

**1** Click the WordArt you want to delete. Handles (O) appear around the WordArt.

**2** Press the Delete key to delete the WordArt.

# ADD AN AUTOSHAPE

Excel provides
ready-made
shapes, called
AutoShapes,
that you can
add to your
worksheet
or chart.

Excel offers
several types
of AutoShapes
such as lines,
arrows, stars
and banners.

## ADD AN AUTOSHAPE

**1** To add an AutoShape
to your worksheet, click
a cell in the worksheet.

■ To add an AutoShape
to a chart, click the chart.

**2** Click 🖉 to display the
Drawing toolbar.

■ The Drawing toolbar
appears.

**3** Click **AutoShapes**.

**4** Click the type of
AutoShape you want
to add.

**5** Click the AutoShape
you want to add.

**Tip**

**Can I add text to an AutoShape?**

You can add text to most AutoShapes. This is particularly useful for AutoShapes such as banners and callouts. To add text to an AutoShape, click the AutoShape and then type the text you want the AutoShape to display.

**Tip**

**How can I change the shape of an AutoShape?**

You can change the shape of any AutoShape that displays a yellow handle ($\diamondsuit$). Click the AutoShape and position the mouse $\triangleright$ over the yellow handle ($\triangleright$ changes to $\triangleright$). Then drag the mouse until the dashed line displays the way you want the AutoShape to appear.

**6** Position the mouse + where you want to begin drawing the AutoShape.

**7** Drag the mouse + until the AutoShape is the size you want.

■ The AutoShape appears. The handles (O) around the AutoShape allow you to change the size of the AutoShape. To move or resize an AutoShape, see page 218.

■ To deselect an AutoShape, click outside the AutoShape.

**DELETE AN AUTOSHAPE**

**1** Click an edge of the AutoShape you want to delete. Handles (O) appear around the AutoShape.

**2** Press the Delete key to delete the AutoShape.

# ADD A TEXT BOX

You can add a
text box to your
worksheet or
chart to display
additional
information.

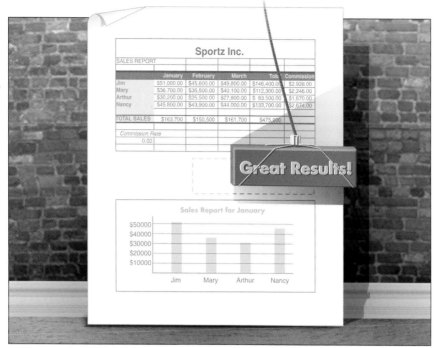

Text boxes are useful
for displaying notes.
You can also use text
boxes to label or
describe items in
your worksheet or
chart.

## ADD A TEXT BOX

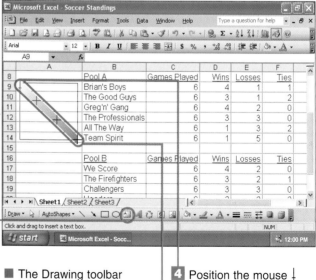

**1** To add a text box to
your worksheet, click a
cell in the worksheet.

■ To add a text box to
a chart, click the chart.

**2** Click 🖎 to display
the Drawing toolbar.

■ The Drawing toolbar
appears.

**3** Click 🖻 to add a
text box.

**4** Position the mouse ↓
where you want to begin
drawing the text box.

**5** Drag the mouse +
until the text box is the
size you want.

To format text, see pages 116 to 126.

 **How do I edit the text in a text box?**

To edit the text in a text box, click the text box and then edit the text as you would edit any text in your worksheet. When you finish editing the text, click outside the text box.

**Tip** **Can I format the text in a text box?**

Yes. Click the text box and then drag the mouse $I$ over the text you want to format until you highlight the text. You can then format the text as you would format any text in your worksheet. For example, you can change the font and size of text or bold, italicize and underline text. To format text, see pages 116 to 126.

■ The text box appears. The handles (O) around the text box allow you to change the size of the text box. To move or resize a text box, see page 218.

**6** Type the text you want the text box to display.

■ To deselect a text box, click outside the text box.

*Note: To hide the Drawing toolbar, repeat step 2.*

DELETE A TEXT BOX

**1** Click an edge of the text box you want to delete. Handles (O) appear around the text box.

**2** Press the `Delete` key to delete the text box.

# ADD A PICTURE

You can add a picture stored on your computer to your worksheet or chart.

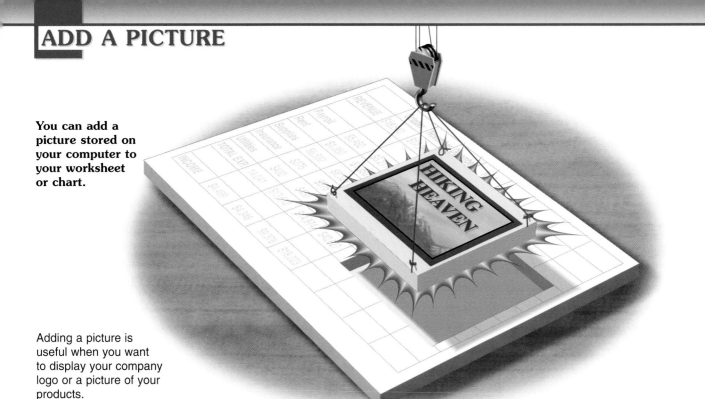

Adding a picture is useful when you want to display your company logo or a picture of your products.

## ADD A PICTURE

**1** To add a picture to your worksheet, click a cell in the worksheet.

■ To add a picture to a chart, click the chart.

**2** Click **Insert**.

**3** Click **Picture**.

**4** Click **From File**.

■ The Insert Picture dialog box appears.

■ This area shows the location of the displayed pictures. You can click this area to change the location.

■ This area allows you to access pictures stored in commonly used locations. You can click a location to display the pictures stored in the location.

*Note: For information on the commonly used locations, see the top of page 23.*

## Where can I get pictures that I can add to my worksheet or chart?

You can purchase collections of pictures at stores that sell computer software or obtain pictures on the Internet. You can also use a scanner to scan pictures into your computer or create your own pictures using an image editing program, such as Adobe Photoshop.

## Why does the Picture toolbar appear when I select a picture in my worksheet or chart?

The Picture toolbar contains buttons that allow you to change the appearance of a picture. For example, you can click one of the following buttons to alter the appearance of a picture.

Increase the brightness of a picture.

Decrease the brightness of a picture.

**5** Click the picture you want to add to your worksheet or chart.

**6** Click **Insert** to add the picture to your worksheet or chart.

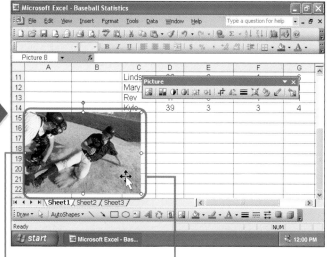

■ The picture appears. The handles (○) around the picture allow you to change the size of the picture. To move or resize a picture, see page 218.

■ To deselect a picture, click outside the picture.

**DELETE A PICTURE**

**1** Click the picture you want to delete. Handles (○) appear around the picture.

**2** Press the Delete key to delete the picture.

# ADD A CLIP ART IMAGE

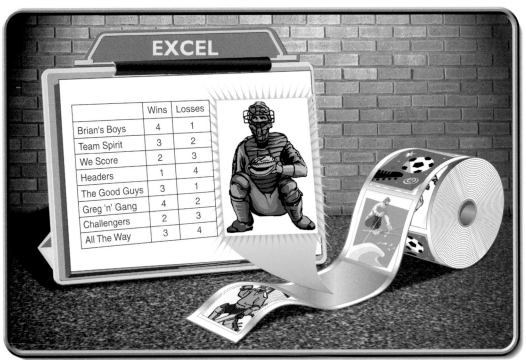

You can add professionally-designed clip art images to your worksheet or chart. Clip art images can help illustrate concepts and make your worksheet or chart more interesting.

## ADD A CLIP ART IMAGE

**1** Click **Insert**.

**2** Click **Picture**.

**3** Click **Clip Art**.

■ The Clip Art task pane appears.

**4** Click **Organize clips** to view all the available clip art images in the Microsoft Clip Organizer.

*Note: The first time you add a clip art image to a worksheet or chart, the Add Clips to Organizer dialog box appears. To catalog the clip art images and other media files on your computer, click **Now** in the dialog box.*

**Tip**

**In the Microsoft Clip Organizer, what type of clip art images will I find in each collection?**

**My Collections**

Displays images that came with Microsoft Windows and images you created or obtained on your own.

**Office Collections**

Displays the images that came with Microsoft Office.

**Web Collections**

Displays the images that are available at Microsoft's Web site and at Web sites in partnership with Microsoft.

■ The Microsoft Clip Organizer window appears.

■ This area displays the folders that contain the clip art images you can add to your worksheet or chart. A folder displaying a plus sign ( ➕ ) contains hidden folders.

**5** To display the hidden folders within a folder, click a plus sign ( ➕ ) beside a folder ( ➕ changes to ➖ ).

*Note: You must be connected to the Internet to view the contents of the Web Collections folder.*

■ The hidden folders appear.

*Note: To once again hide the folders within a folder, click a minus sign ( ➖ ) beside a folder.*

**6** Click a folder of interest.

■ This area displays the contents of the folder you selected.

**7** Click the clip art image you want to add.

**CONTINUED** ▶

# ADD A CLIP ART IMAGE

After you locate an image you want to add to your worksheet or chart, you can copy the image to the clipboard and then place the image in your worksheet or chart.

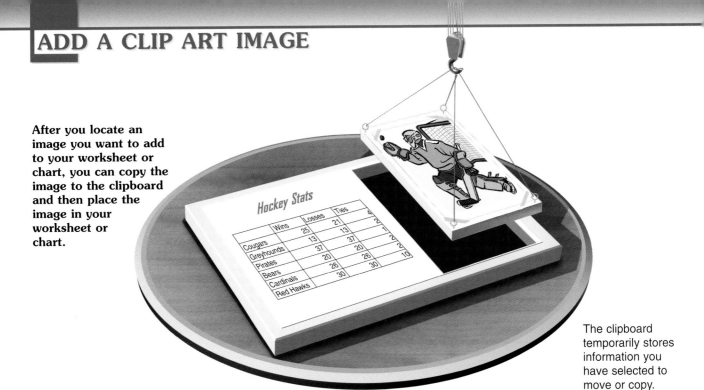

The clipboard temporarily stores information you have selected to move or copy.

**8** Click to copy the image you selected to the clipboard.

**9** Click ✕ to close the Microsoft Clip Organizer window.

■ A dialog box appears, stating that you have one or more clip art images on the clipboard.

**10** Click **Yes** to keep the image on the clipboard.

**11** To add the image to your worksheet, click a cell in the worksheet.

■ To add the image to a chart, click the chart.

**12** Click to place the image in your worksheet or chart.

■ The clip art image appears. The handles ( O ) around the clip art image allow you to change the size of the image. To move or resize an image, see page 218.

216

**Tip**

**Where can I obtain more clip art images?**

You can buy collections of clip art images at computer stores. Many Web sites, such as www.noeticart.com, also offer clip art images you can use in your worksheet or chart.

 **Tip**

**How do I delete a clip art image?**

To delete a clip art image, click the clip art image and then press the Delete key.

## SEARCH FOR A CLIP ART IMAGE

**You can search for clip art images by specifying one or more words of interest in the Clip Art task pane.**

*Note: To display the Clip Art task pane, perform steps 1 to 3 on page 214.*

■ This area displays the images that match the words you specified.

**3** Click the image you want to add to your worksheet or chart.

**1** Click this area and then type one or more words that describe the clip art image you want to find. Then press the Enter key.

**2** To add an image to your worksheet, click a cell in the worksheet.

■ To add an image to a chart, click the chart.

■ The image appears in your worksheet or chart.

217

# MOVE OR RESIZE AN OBJECT

You can change the
location and size of
an object in your
worksheet or chart.

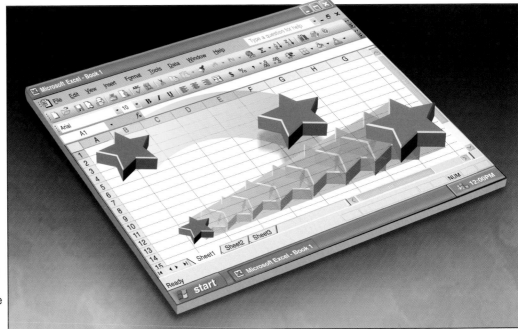

For example, you may
want to move a picture
to a more suitable
location or increase the
size of a text box to
display more text.

## MOVE AN OBJECT

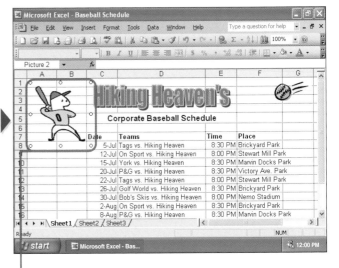

**1** Click the object you want
to move. Handles (○)
appear around the object.

**2** Position the mouse ⬚
over an edge of the object
(⬚ changes to ✛).

**3** Drag the object
to a new location.

■ A dashed line
indicates where the
object will appear.

■ The object appears in
the new location.

*Note: If the object you are
moving is on a chart, you
cannot move the object outside
the chart area.*

■ To deselect the object,
click outside the object.

**Tip**

**Which handle (○) should I use to resize an object?**

The handles that appear at the top and bottom of an object (●) allow you to change the height of the object. The handles at the sides of an object (●) allow you to change the width of the object. The handles at the corners of an object (●) allow you to change the height and width of the object at the same time.

**Tip**

**How can I change the way an object is moved or resized?**

To move an object only horizontally or vertically, press and hold down the `Shift` key as you move the object.

To keep the center of an object in the same place while resizing the object, press and hold down the `Ctrl` key as you resize the object.

## RESIZE AN OBJECT

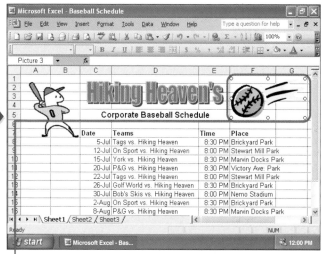

**1** Click the object you want to resize. Handles (○) appear around the object.

**2** Position the mouse ⊹ over one of the handles (⊹ changes to ↗, ↘, ↔ or ↕).

**3** Drag the handle until the object is the size you want.

■ A dashed line indicates the new size.

■ The object appears in the new size.

■ To deselect the object, click outside the object.

# CHANGE THE COLOR OF AN OBJECT

You can change the color of an object in your worksheet or chart.

You cannot change the color of some clip art images and pictures.

## CHANGE THE COLOR OF AN OBJECT

**1** Click an edge of the object you want to change to a different color. Handles (○) appear around the object.

**2** Click 🖼 to display the Drawing toolbar.

**3** Click ▾ in this area to display the available colors.

**4** Click the color you want to use.

■ The object appears in the color you selected.

■ To deselect an object, click outside the object.

*Note: To hide the Drawing toolbar, repeat step 2.*

220

# ROTATE AN OBJECT

You can rotate
an object in
your worksheet
or chart.

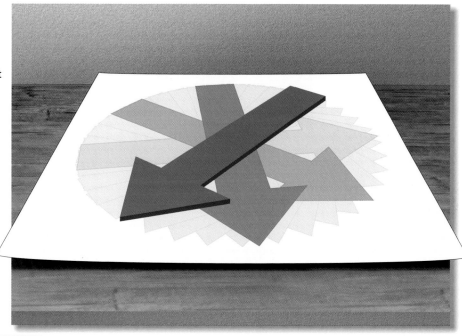

You cannot
rotate text boxes
and some
AutoShapes.

## ROTATE AN OBJECT

**1** Click the object you
want to rotate. Handles (O)
appear around the object.

**2** Position the mouse ⬚
over the green dot
(⬚ changes to ↻).

**3** Drag the mouse ◌
in the direction you
want to rotate the object.

■ The object appears
in the new position.

■ To deselect an object,
click outside the object.

# ADD A SHADOW TO AN OBJECT

You can add a shadow to add depth to an object in your worksheet or chart.

## ADD A SHADOW TO AN OBJECT

**1** Click the object you want to display a shadow.

**2** Click 🎨 to display the Drawing toolbar.

**3** Click 🔲 to display the available shadow styles.

**4** Click the shadow style you want to use.

*Note: If a shadow style is dimmed, the style is not available for the object you selected.*

■ The object displays the shadow.

*Note: To hide the Drawing toolbar, repeat step 2.*

■ To remove a shadow from an object, repeat steps **1** to **4**, selecting **No Shadow** in step **4**.

You can make
an object in your
worksheet or
chart appear
three-dimensional.

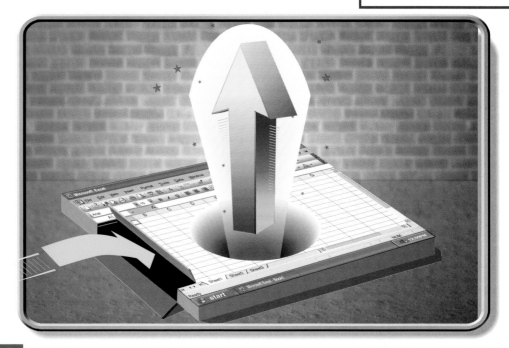

## MAKE AN OBJECT 3-D

**1** Click the object you want
to appear three-dimensional.

**2** Click 🔲 to display the
Drawing toolbar.

**3** Click 🔲 to display
the available 3-D effects.

**4** Click the 3-D effect
you want to use.

*Note: If the 3-D effects are
dimmed, you cannot make
the object you selected
three-dimensional.*

■ The object displays
the 3-D effect.

*Note: To hide the Drawing
toolbar, repeat step 2.*

■ To remove a 3-D effect
from an object, repeat
steps **1** to **4**, selecting
**No 3-D** in step **4**.

# ADD A DIAGRAM

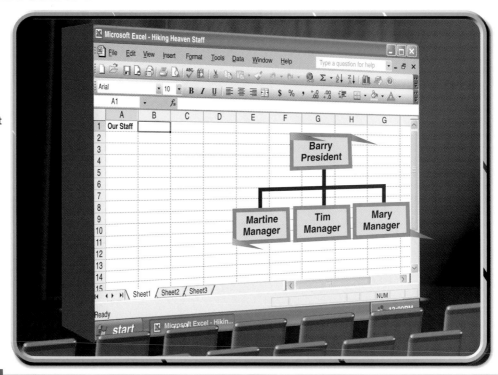

You can add a diagram to a worksheet to illustrate a concept or idea. Excel provides several types of diagrams for you to choose from.

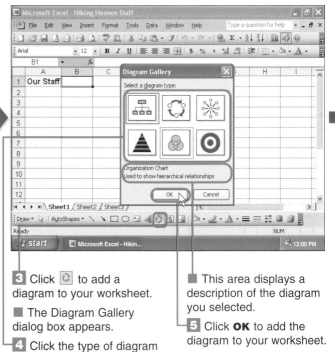

**1** To add a diagram to your worksheet, click a cell in the worksheet.

**2** Click ![icon] to display the Drawing toolbar.

■ The Drawing toolbar appears.

**3** Click ![icon] to add a diagram to your worksheet.

■ The Diagram Gallery dialog box appears.

**4** Click the type of diagram you want to add.

■ This area displays a description of the diagram you selected.

**5** Click **OK** to add the diagram to your worksheet.

## Tip

**What types of diagrams can I add to my worksheet?**

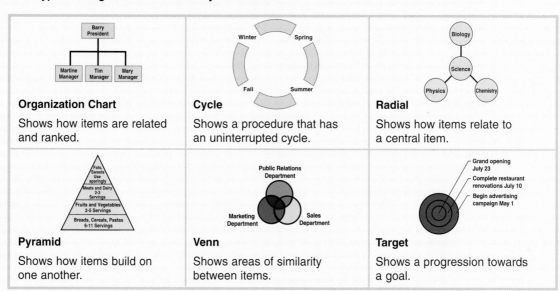

**Organization Chart**

Shows how items are related and ranked.

**Cycle**

Shows a procedure that has an uninterrupted cycle.

**Radial**

Shows how items relate to a central item.

**Pyramid**

Shows how items build on one another.

**Venn**

Shows areas of similarity between items.

**Target**

Shows a progression towards a goal.

■ The diagram appears in your worksheet.

*Note: You can resize the diagram the same way you would resize any object.*

■ A toolbar also appears, displaying buttons that allow you to change the diagram.

■ To deselect a diagram, click outside the diagram.

*Note: To hide the Drawing toolbar, repeat step 2.*

**ADD TEXT**

**1** Click an area where you want to add text.

■ A border appears around the area if you can add text to the area.

**2** Type the text you want to add.

**3** When you finish typing the text, click outside the text area.

■ Repeat steps **1** to **3** for each area of text you want to add.

**CONTINUED**

# ADD A DIAGRAM

You can add
a new shape
to a diagram
to include
additional
information
in the diagram.

## ADD A DIAGRAM (CONTINUED)

### ADD A SHAPE

**1** Click the shape above or beside where you want the new shape to appear.

**2** To add a shape to an organization chart, click ⦁ beside **Insert Shape**.

**3** Click the option that describes where you want to position the shape.

■ To add a shape to all other types of diagrams, click **Insert Shape**.

■ The new shape appears in the diagram.

■ You can add text to the new shape.

■ To delete a shape, click an edge of the shape you want to delete and then press the Delete key.

**Tip**

**Where can I position a shape I add to an organization chart?**

**Subordinate**
Adds a shape below the shape you selected.

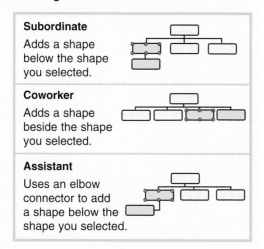

**Coworker**
Adds a shape beside the shape you selected.

**Assistant**
Uses an elbow connector to add a shape below the shape you selected.

**Tip**

**How do I delete a diagram?**

**1** To delete a diagram, click the diagram you want to delete.

■ A border appears around the diagram.

**2** Click the border and then press the Delete key.

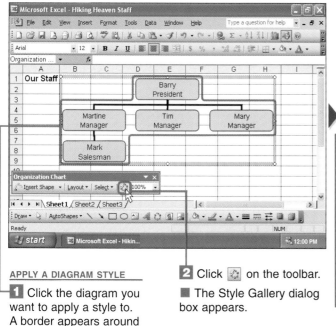

APPLY A DIAGRAM STYLE

**1** Click the diagram you want to apply a style to. A border appears around the diagram.

**2** Click 🔅 on the toolbar.

■ The Style Gallery dialog box appears.

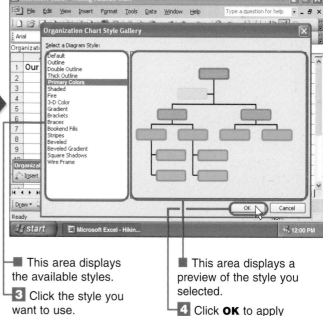

■ This area displays the available styles.

**3** Click the style you want to use.

■ This area displays a preview of the style you selected.

**4** Click **OK** to apply the style to the diagram.

■ To remove a diagram style, repeat steps **1** to **4**, selecting **Default** in step **3**.

| Player | RBIs | Home Runs | |
|--------|------|-----------|---|
| | | | 1 |
| | | 5 | 1 |
| Barry | 56 | 6 | 1 |
| Martine | 51 | 2 | |
| | | | 2 |
| Lindsay | 32 | 8 | 3 |
| Mary | 48 | 3 | |
| Kyle | 39 | | |
| * | | | 8 |
| | | 24 | |
| Total | 226 | | |

## CHAPTER 12

# Manage Data in a List

*Would you like Excel to help you organize a large collection of data? In this chapter, you will learn how to sort data in a list, add totals to a list and more.*

# CREATE A LIST

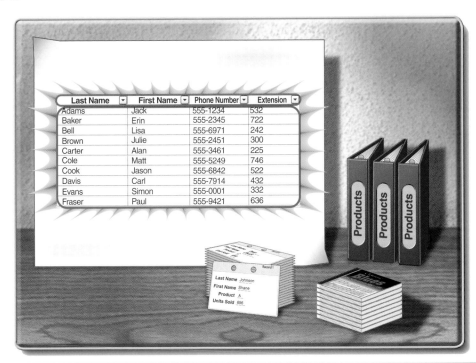

You can create a list to organize a large collection of data, such as a mailing list, phone directory, product list or music collection.

The first row in a list contains the **column labels** for the list. A column label, also called a header, describes the data in a column. Each row in a list contains one **record**. A record is a group of related data.

## CREATE A LIST

**1** Type the column labels that describe the data you will enter into each column.

**2** Enter the data for each record.

*Note: For guidelines on creating a list, see the top of page 231.*

**3** Select the cells containing the column labels and data you want to include in the list. To select cells, see page 10.

**4** Click **Data**.

**5** Click **List**.

**6** Click **Create List**.

**Tip**

**What should I consider when creating a list?**

➤ Do not include blank rows or columns in the list.

➤ Keep the list separate from other data or lists on the worksheet. For example, leave a blank row or column between the list and other items.

➤ When entering data into a cell in the list, avoid entering blank spaces at the beginning or end of the data.

**Tip**

**Can I quickly print a list I have created?**

Yes. You can quickly print only the data in your list, without printing any other data in your worksheet. Click a cell in the list to make the list active. On the List toolbar, click ![icon] to quickly print your list. If the List toolbar is not displayed, see page 111 to display the toolbar.

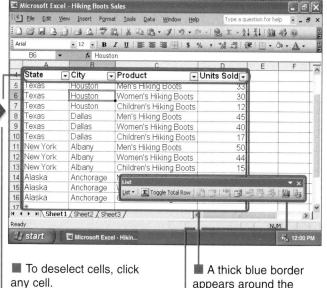

■ The Create List dialog box appears.

■ This area displays the range of cells you selected to include in the list.

■ This option specifies that your list includes column labels. You can click the option to turn the option on (☑) or off (☐).

**7** Click **OK** to create the list.

■ To deselect cells, click any cell.

■ The column labels in the list appear in **bold** type. An arrow (▼) also appears beside each column label in the list.

■ A thick blue border appears around the outside of the list.

■ The List toolbar appears on your screen, containing tools you can use to work with the list.

# ADD A RECORD

You can add a record to include additional data in your list at any time.

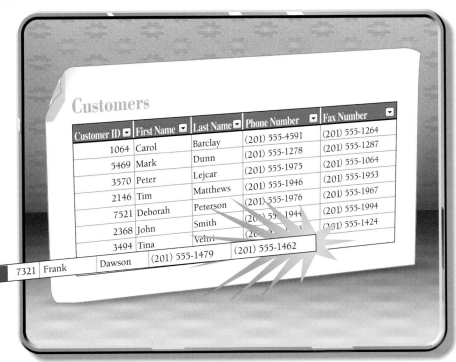

Customers

| Customer ID | First Name | Last Name | Phone Number | Fax Number |
|---|---|---|---|---|
| 1064 | Carol | Barclay | (201) 555-4591 | (201) 555-1264 |
| 5469 | Mark | Dunn | (201) 555-1278 | (201) 555-1287 |
| 3570 | Peter | Lejcar | (201) 555-1975 | (201) 555-1064 |
| 2146 | Tim | Matthews | (201) 555-1946 | (201) 555-1953 |
| 7521 | Deborah | Peterson | (201) 555-1976 | (201) 555-1967 |
| 2368 | John | Smith | (201) 555-1944 | (201) 555-1994 |
| 3494 | Tina | Veltri | (20 ) 55 | (201) 555-1424 |
| 7321 | Frank | Dawson | (201) 555-1479 | (201) 555-1462 |

When adding a record to a list, you enter the data for the record at the end of the list. If you later want to change the order of the records in the list, you can sort the records. To sort records, see page 234.

## ADD A RECORD

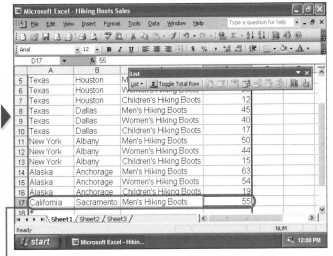

**1** Click a cell in the list to make the list active.

*Note: An active list displays a thick blue border and arrows ( ▾ ) beside the column labels.*

**2** Click the cell that displays the ✳ symbol.

**3** Type the data that corresponds to the first column and then press the `Tab` key. Repeat this step until you have entered all the data for the record.

### EDIT DATA

■ You can edit data for a record directly in your list to update or correct the data. To edit data, see page 38.

# DELETE A RECORD

You can delete a record to remove data you no longer need from the list. For example, you may want to remove information about a customer who no longer orders your products.

Deleting records keeps your list from becoming cluttered with unnecessary information.

## DELETE A RECORD

**1** Select the cells that contain the record you want to delete. To select cells, see page 10.

**2** Click **Edit**.

**3** Click **Delete Row** to delete the row containing the record from the list.

■ The row disappears and all the rows that follow shift upward.

*Note: Deleting a row from a list does not affect data in the same row that is not part of the list.*

■ To deselect a row, click any cell.

### DELETE DATA

■ You can delete data from a record directly in your list. To delete data, see page 40.

233

# SORT DATA IN A LIST

You can change the order of records in a list. This can help you organize and analyze data.

## SORT BY ONE COLUMN

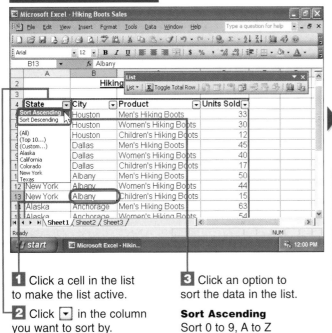

**1** Click a cell in the list to make the list active.

**2** Click ▾ in the column you want to sort by.

**3** Click an option to sort the data in the list.

**Sort Ascending**
Sort 0 to 9, A to Z

**Sort Descending**
Sort 9 to 0, Z to A

■ The records in the list appear in the new order.

■ In this example, the records are sorted by state.

■ To immediately reverse the results of sorting records, click ↺.

*Note: If ↺ is not displayed, click ⁑ on the Standard toolbar to display the button.*

**Tip**

**Why would I sort my list by more than one column?**

Sorting by more than one column allows you to further organize the data in your list. For example, if a last name appears more than once in the Last Name column, you can sort by a second column, such as the First Name column.

## SORT BY TWO COLUMNS

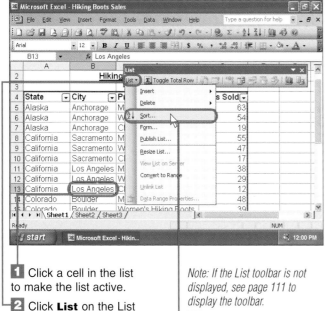

**1** Click a cell in the list to make the list active.

**2** Click **List** on the List toolbar.

*Note: If the List toolbar is not displayed, see page 111 to display the toolbar.*

**3** Click **Sort**.

■ The Sort dialog box appears.

**4** Click ⊻ in this area to select the first column you want to sort by.

**5** Click the name of the first column you want to sort by.

**CONTINUED**

# SORT DATA IN A LIST

You can sort the records in your list by letter, number or date.

**LETTER**
A
B
C
D
E
F
G
H

**NUMBER**
100
200
300
400
500
600
700
800

**DATE**
Jan-01
Feb-01
Mar-01
Apr-01
May-01
Jun-01
Jul-01
Aug-01

## SORT BY TWO COLUMNS (CONTINUED)

**6** Click an option to specify the way you want to sort the first column ( ○ changes to ⊙ ).

**Ascending**
Sort 0 to 9, A to Z

**Descending**
Sort 9 to 0, Z to A

**7** Click ⌄ in this area to select the second column you want to sort by.

**8** Click the name of the column you want to sort by.

## Tip

**How often can I sort the records in my list?**

You can sort the records in your list as often as you like. Sorting is useful if you frequently add new records to your list.

## Tip

**How will Excel sort records if I sort by a column that contains blank cells?**

If you sort by a column that contains blank cells, Excel will place the records containing the blank cells at the end of your list.

■ **9** Click an option to specify the way you want to sort the second column ( ○ changes to ◉ ).

■ **10** Click **OK** to sort the records.

■ The records in the list appear in the new order.

■ In this example, the records are sorted by state. When a state appears more than once in the list, the records are then sorted by city.

■ To immediately reverse the results of sorting records, click 🔄 .

*Note: If 🔄 is not displayed, click ⏬ on the Standard toolbar to display the button.*

# DISPLAY A TOTAL ROW

You can display a Total row at the bottom of your list to display the results of common calculations in your list. For example, you can display the sum of a column of numbers or the number of records in the list.

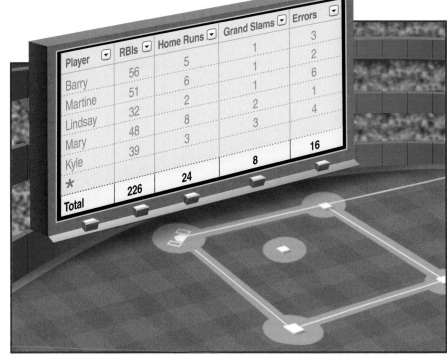

You can display the result of a calculation for any column in your list.

## DISPLAY A TOTAL ROW

**1** Click a cell in the list to make the list active.

**2** Click **Toggle Total Row** on the List toolbar.

*Note: If the List toolbar is not displayed, see page 111 to display the toolbar.*

■ A Total row appears at the bottom of your list.

■ The first cell in the row displays the word "Total." The last cell in the row displays a total of the items in the last column.

**3** In the Total row, click a cell that you want to display the result of a calculation, An arrow ▾ appears beside the cell.

**4** Click ▾ to display a list of common calculations.

**5** Click the calculation you want to perform.

■ The cell will display the result of the calculation you selected.

*Note: To once again hide the Total row, repeat step 2.*

You can filter
your list to
display only
the records
containing the
data you want
to review.

Excel allows you
to analyze your
data by placing
related records
together and
hiding the records
you do not want
to review.

## FILTER A LIST

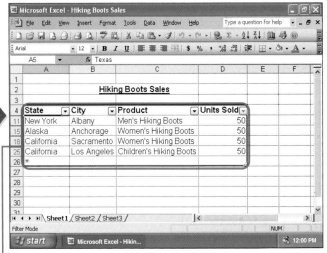

**1** Click a cell in the list to
make the list active.

**2** Click ⏷ in the
column containing the
data you want to use to
filter the list.

**3** Click the data you
want to use to filter the
list.

■ The list displays only the
records containing the data
you specified. The other
records are temporarily
hidden.

■ In this example, the list
displays only the records for
products that sold 50 units.

**REDISPLAY ALL RECORDS**

■ To redisplay all the
records, perform steps **2**
and **3** in the column you
used to filter the list, except
click **(All)** in
step **3**.

**CONTINUED** ▶

# FILTER A LIST

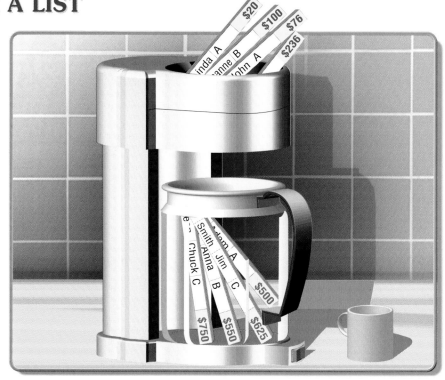

You can filter your list to display only records containing data within a specific range.

For example, you can display records for employees whose sales are greater than or equal to $500.

## FILTER A LIST BY COMPARING DATA

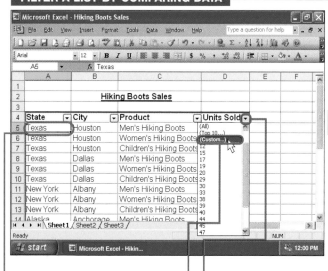

**1** Click a cell in the list to make the list active.

**2** Click ⏷ in the column containing the data you want to use to filter the list.

**3** Click **(Custom...)**.

■ The Custom AutoFilter dialog box appears.

**4** Type the data you want Excel to compare to each record in the list.

**Tip**

### How can I compare data in my list?

Excel offers many ways you can compare data to help you analyze the data in your list.

equals
does not equal
is greater than
is greater than or equal to
is less than
is less than or equal to
begins with
does not begin with
ends with
does not end with
contains
does not contain

**Tip**

### How can I use the (Blanks) and (NonBlanks) options to filter my list?

The (Blanks) and (NonBlanks) options are available when you filter a list using a column that contains blank cells. You can select the (Blanks) option to display only the records containing blank cells. You can select the (NonBlanks) option to display only the records without blank cells.

**Filter by: (Blanks)**

| HIKING BOOT SALES | | |
|---|---|---|
| State | Product | Units Sold |
| New York | Men's Hiking Boots | 50 |
| | Women's Hiking Boots | |
| | Children's Hiking Boots | 109 |
| Florida | Men's Hiking Boots | 64 |
| | Women's Hiking Boots | |
| | Children's Hiking Boots | 77 |
| Texas | Men's Hiking Boots | |
| | Women's Hiking Boots | 13 |
| | Children's Hiking Boots | 4 |

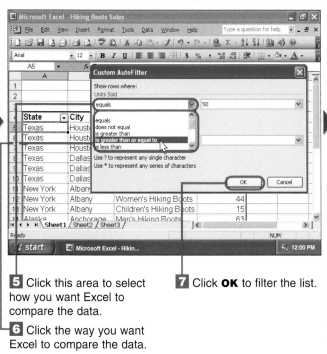

**5** Click this area to select how you want Excel to compare the data.

**6** Click the way you want Excel to compare the data.

**7** Click **OK** to filter the list.

■ The list displays only the records containing the data you specified. The other records are temporarily hidden.

■ In this example, the list displays only the records for products that sold 50 units or more.

**REDISPLAY ALL RECORDS**

■ To redisplay all the records, perform steps **2** and **3** in the column you used to filter the list, except click **(All)** in step **3**.

## CHAPTER 13

# Protect Your Data

*Do you want to prevent other people from making changes to your workbooks or worksheets? Learn how in this chapter.*

# PROTECT A WORKBOOK

You can prevent other people from opening or making changes to a workbook by protecting it with a password.

You should save a workbook before protecting it with a password. To save a workbook, see page 22.

## PROTECT A WORKBOOK

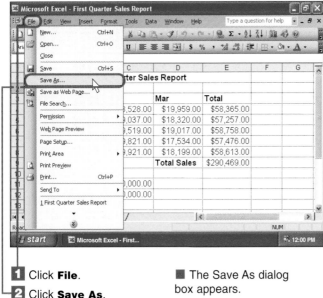

**1** Click **File**.

**2** Click **Save As**.

■ The Save As dialog box appears.

**3** Click **Tools**.

**4** Click **General Options**.

■ The Save Options dialog box appears.

**Tip**

### What password should I use to protect my workbook?

When choosing a password, you should not use words that people can easily associate with you, such as your name or favorite sport. The most effective passwords connect two words or numbers with a special character (example: **car#123**). A password can contain up to 15 characters and be any combination of letters, numbers and symbols.

**Tip**

### Should I take any special precautions with my password?

You should write down your password and keep it in a safe place. If you forget the password, you may not be able to open the workbook.

**5** Click the box for the type of password you want to enter.

**Password to open**

Prevents people from opening the workbook without entering the correct password.

**Password to modify**

Prevents people from making changes to the workbook without entering the correct password.

**6** Type the password you want to use.

**7** Click **OK** to continue.

**CONTINUED**

# PROTECT A WORKBOOK

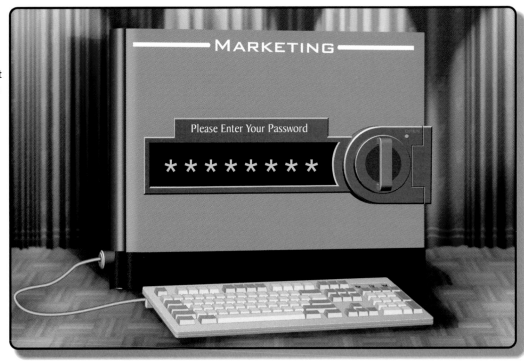

After you protect
a workbook with
a password,
Excel will ask
you to enter the
password each
time you open
the workbook.

PROTECT A WORKBOOK (CONTINUED)

■ The Confirm Password
dialog box appears,
asking you to confirm the
password you entered.

**8** Type the password
again to confirm the
password.

**9** Click **OK** to protect
the workbook.

**10** Click **Save** in the
Save As dialog box.

■ A dialog box appears,
stating that you are about
to replace the existing file.

**11** Click **Yes** to replace the
file and save the workbook
with the password.

Protect
Your Data **13**

**Tip**

**I typed the correct password, but Excel will not open my workbook. What is wrong?**

Passwords in Excel are case sensitive. If you do not enter the correct uppercase and lowercase letters, Excel will not accept the password. For example, if your password is **car#123**, you cannot enter **Car#123** or **CAR#123** to open the workbook.

**Tip**

**How do I unprotect a workbook?**

To unprotect a workbook, perform steps **1** to **7** starting on page 244, except in step **6**, drag the mouse I over the existing password until you highlight the password and then press the Delete key. Then perform steps **10** and **11**.

---

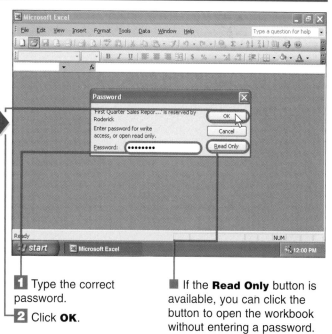

**OPEN A PROTECTED WORKBOOK**

■ A Password dialog box appears each time you open a protected workbook. To open a workbook, see page 32.

*Note: The appearance of the dialog box depends on the type of password assigned to the workbook.*

**1** Type the correct password.

**2** Click **OK**.

■ If the **Read Only** button is available, you can click the button to open the workbook without entering a password. You will not be able to save changes you make to the workbook.

# PROTECT WORKBOOK ELEMENTS

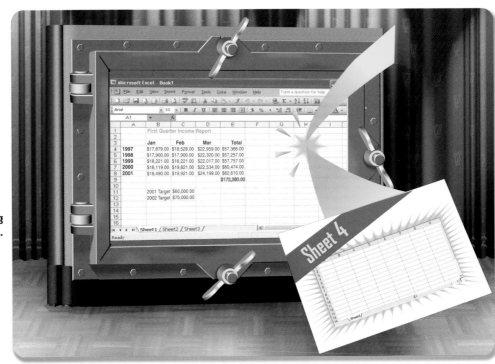

You can prevent people from changing the structure of a workbook and the way the workbook window is displayed. For example, you can prevent people from inserting a new worksheet into a workbook and resizing the workbook window.

## PROTECT WORKBOOK ELEMENTS

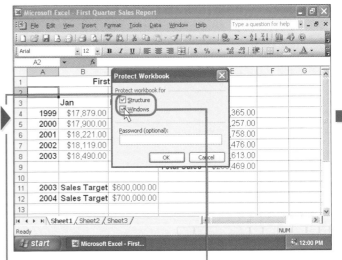

**1** Click **Tools**.

**2** Click **Protection**.

**3** Click **Protect Workbook**.

■ The Protect Workbook dialog box appears.

■ This area displays the workbook elements Excel can protect.

■ A check mark (✔) beside an element indicates that Excel will prevent people from changing the element.

**4** You can click the box beside an element to add ( ☑ ) or remove ( ☐ ) a check mark.

## Tip

**What workbook elements can Excel protect?**

**Structure**

Prevents people from renaming, inserting, deleting, moving or copying worksheets in a workbook.

**Windows**

Prevents people from moving, resizing or closing the window for a workbook.

## Tip

**How do I unprotect workbook elements?**

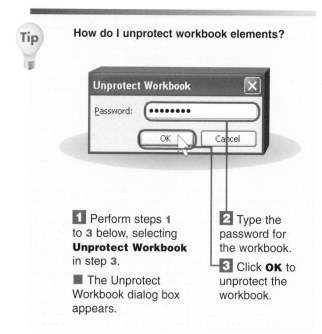

**1** Perform steps **1** to **3** below, selecting **Unprotect Workbook** in step **3**.

■ The Unprotect Workbook dialog box appears.

**2** Type the password for the workbook.

**3** Click **OK** to unprotect the workbook.

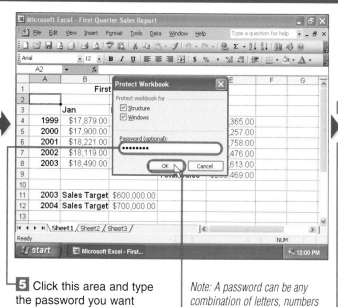

**5** Click this area and type the password you want people to enter to unprotect workbook elements.

*Note: A password can be any combination of letters, numbers and symbols.*

**6** Click **OK** to continue.

■ The Confirm Password dialog box appears, asking you to confirm the password you entered.

**7** Type the password again to confirm the password.

**8** Click **OK** to protect the workbook.

# PROTECT A WORKSHEET

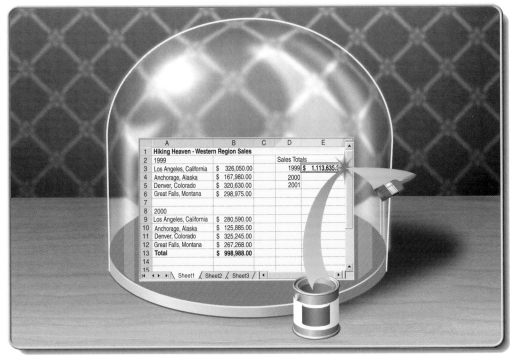

You can prevent other people from making changes to your worksheet. This helps to prevent other users from accidentally making changes to your data while reviewing your worksheet.

## PROTECT A WORKSHEET

**1** Display the worksheet you want to protect. To switch between worksheets, see page 170.

**2** Click **Tools**.

**3** Click **Protection**.

**4** Click **Protect Sheet**.

■ The Protect Sheet dialog box appears.

**5** Click this area and type the password you want people to enter to unprotect your worksheet.

*Note: A password can be any combination of letters, numbers and symbols.*

**What are some of the tasks I can allow people to perform in my protected worksheet?**

| Format Cells | Allow people to change the formatting of data in cells, such as the font or style. |
| --- | --- |
| Format Columns | Allow people to change the width of columns and hide columns. |
| Insert Columns | Allow people to insert columns. |
| Delete Columns | Allow people to delete columns. |
| Sort | Allow people to sort data. |
| Edit Objects | Allow people to change objects such as charts, AutoShapes and text boxes. |

**How do I unprotect a worksheet?**

■ Display the worksheet you want to unprotect. To switch between worksheets, see page 170.

② Perform steps 2 to 4 below, selecting **Unprotect sheet** in step 4.

■ The Unprotect Sheet dialog box appears.

③ Type the password for the worksheet.

④ Click **OK** to unprotect the worksheet.

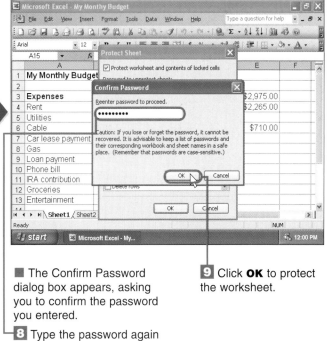

■ This area displays the tasks that you can allow people to perform in your protected worksheet. A check mark (✔) beside a task indicates that Excel will allow people to perform the task.

⑥ You can click the box beside a task to add (☑) or remove (☐) a check mark.

⑦ Click **OK** to continue.

■ The Confirm Password dialog box appears, asking you to confirm the password you entered.

⑧ Type the password again to confirm the password.

⑨ Click **OK** to protect the worksheet.

## CHAPTER 14

# Time-Saving Features

*Would you like to learn how to customize Excel to help you save time? In this chapter, you will learn how to create your own toolbar, use smart tags to perform tasks and much more.*

# CREATE A CUSTOM SERIES

You can create a custom series that you can quickly enter into your worksheets. Creating a custom series is useful if you frequently enter the same data, such as a list of employee names.

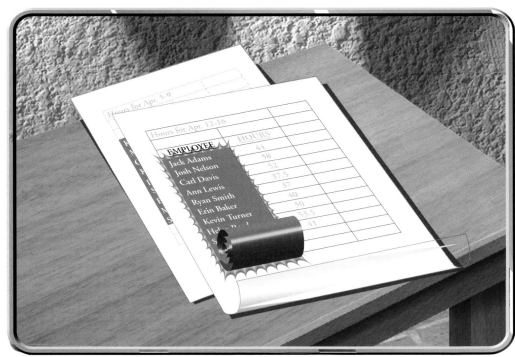

## CREATE A CUSTOM SERIES

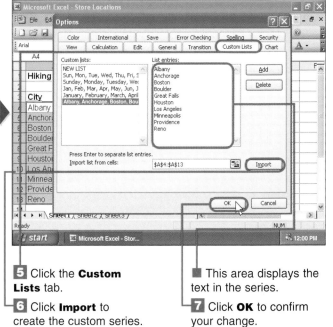

**1** Enter the text you want to save as a series.

■ To include numbers in a series, you must first format the cells that will contain the numbers as text. To format cells as text, see page 134.

**2** Select the cells containing the text you entered. To select cells, see page 10.

**3** Click **Tools**.

**4** Click **Options**.

■ The Options dialog box appears.

**5** Click the **Custom Lists** tab.

**6** Click **Import** to create the custom series.

■ This area displays the text in the series.

**7** Click **OK** to confirm your change.

**Tip**

**How do I complete a custom series that begins with a number?**

If the first item in a custom series is a number, you must format the cell that will contain the number as text before performing steps **1** to **4** on page 255. To format cells as text, see page 134.

**Tip**

**When creating a custom series that contains numbers, why do green triangles appear in the cells I formatted as text?**

Excel displays green triangles in the top left corner of cells that may contain errors, such as cells formatted as text that contain numbers.

**1** To remove a green triangle from a cell, click the cell.

■ The Trace Error button (⊠) appears.

**2** Click the Trace Error button to display a list of options.

**3** Click **Ignore Error**.

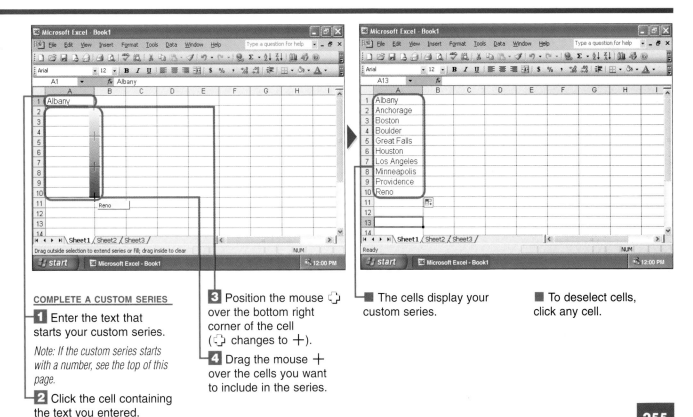

**COMPLETE A CUSTOM SERIES**

**1** Enter the text that starts your custom series.

*Note: If the custom series starts with a number, see the top of this page.*

**2** Click the cell containing the text you entered.

**3** Position the mouse ⬦ over the bottom right corner of the cell (⬦ changes to +).

**4** Drag the mouse + over the cells you want to include in the series.

■ The cells display your custom series.

■ To deselect cells, click any cell.

# CUSTOMIZE A TOOLBAR

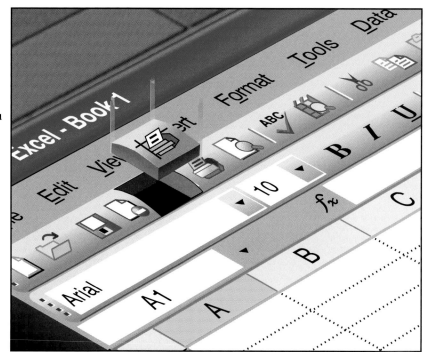

You can add buttons to a toolbar to provide quick access to the commands you use most often. This can help you work more efficiently.

Excel offers hundreds of buttons for you to choose from.

To display a toolbar, see page 111.

## ADD A BUTTON

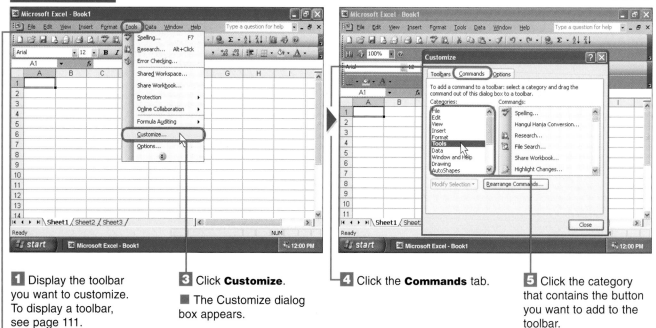

**1** Display the toolbar you want to customize. To display a toolbar, see page 111.

**2** Click **Tools**.

**3** Click **Customize**.

■ The Customize dialog box appears.

**4** Click the **Commands** tab.

**5** Click the category that contains the button you want to add to the toolbar.

**Tip**

**I don't like my customized toolbar. How can I return the toolbar to its original appearance?**

**1** Perform steps **2** and **3** below to display the Customize dialog box.

**2** Click the **Toolbars** tab.

**3** Click the name of the toolbar you want to return to its original appearance.

**4** Click **Reset**.

**5** In the confirmation dialog box that appears, click **OK** to undo all the changes you have made to the toolbar.

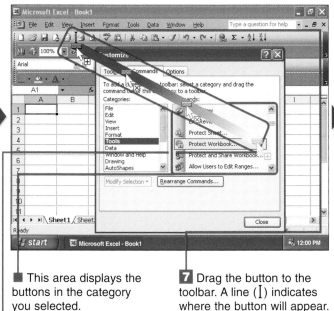

■ This area displays the buttons in the category you selected.

**6** Position the mouse over the button you want to add to the toolbar.

**7** Drag the button to the toolbar. A line ([) indicates where the button will appear.

■ The button appears on the toolbar.

■ You can repeat steps **5** to **7** for each button you want to add to the toolbar.

**8** When you finish adding buttons to the toolbar, click **Close** to close the Customize dialog box.

**CONTINUED**

# CUSTOMIZE A TOOLBAR

You can move buttons on a toolbar to place buttons for related tasks together. This can make it easier to find the buttons you need.

## MOVE A BUTTON

**1** Display the toolbar you want to customize. To display a toolbar, see page 111.

**2** Position the mouse over the button you want to move to a new location.

**3** Hold down the Alt key as you drag the button to a new location. A line ( I ) indicates where the button will appear.

■ The button appears in the new location on the toolbar.

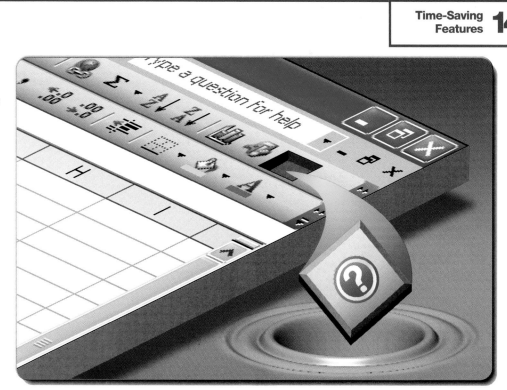

You can remove
buttons you do
not use from a
toolbar.

## REMOVE A BUTTON

**1** Display the toolbar
you want to customize.
To display a toolbar,
see page 111.

**2** Position the mouse ⌖
over the button you want
to remove from the toolbar.

**3** Press and hold down
the **Alt** key as you drag
the button downward off
the toolbar.

■ The button disappears
from the toolbar.

# CREATE A NEW TOOLBAR

You can create a new toolbar containing buttons you frequently use.

Creating a toolbar allows you to have a specific toolbar for a task you regularly perform, such as printing workbooks or adding AutoShapes.

## CREATE A NEW TOOLBAR

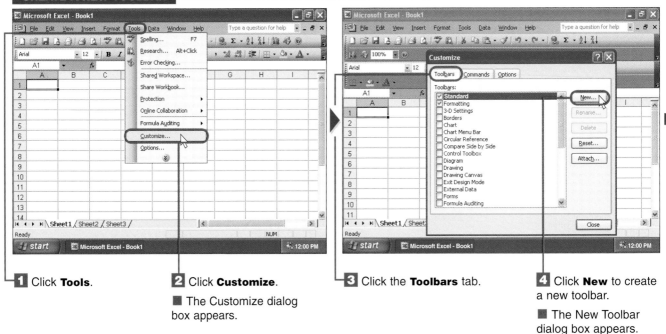

**1** Click **Tools**.

**2** Click **Customize**.

■ The Customize dialog box appears.

**3** Click the **Toolbars** tab.

**4** Click **New** to create a new toolbar.

■ The New Toolbar dialog box appears.

**Tip**

**How can I move a toolbar I created?**

After you create a new toolbar, you can move the toolbar to a new location on your screen. To move a toolbar, position the mouse ⍦ over the title bar and then drag the toolbar to a new location ( ⍦ changes to ✛ ).

**Tip**

**How can I hide a toolbar I created?**

You can hide or display a toolbar you created as you would any toolbar. To hide or display a toolbar, see page 111.

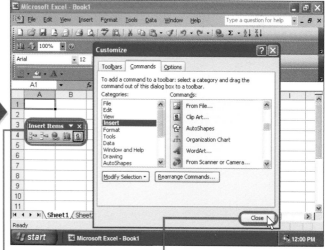

**5** Type a name for the toolbar.

**6** Click **OK** to create the toolbar.

■ The new toolbar appears on your screen.

**7** You can now add the buttons you want the toolbar to display. To add buttons to a toolbar, see page 256.

*Note: You can also move or remove buttons on the toolbar. To move or remove buttons on a toolbar, see page 258 or 259.*

**8** When you finish adding buttons to the toolbar, click **Close** to close the Customize dialog box.

# TURN ON SMART TAGS

You can use smart tags to perform actions in Excel that you would normally have to open another program to perform, such as scheduling a meeting or displaying stock information. Before you can use smart tags in Excel, you must turn on smart tags.

After you turn on smart tags, smart tags will be available in all your workbooks.

## TURN ON SMART TAGS

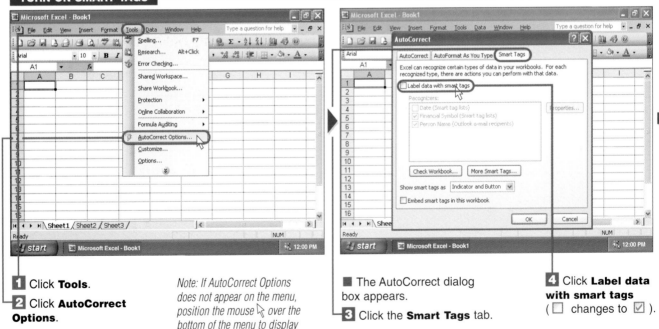

**1** Click **Tools**.

**2** Click **AutoCorrect Options**.

*Note: If AutoCorrect Options does not appear on the menu, position the mouse ℞ over the bottom of the menu to display the menu option.*

■ The AutoCorrect dialog box appears.

**3** Click the **Smart Tags** tab.

**4** Click **Label data with smart tags** ( □ changes to ☑ ).

**Tip**

## What types of data can Excel label with a smart tag?

### Date

Excel can label dates you type, such as 12/23/2003 or 4/21/2004.

| ress | Date |
|------|------|
| Beach St. | 12/23/2003 |
| Pine St. | 04/21/2004 |
| Westside St. | 11/07/2003 |

Calendar
August 2004

### Financial Symbol

Excel can label financial symbols you type in capital letters. For example:

| To obtain information about: | Type: |
|------------------------------|-------|
| Microsoft Corporation | MSFT |
| Intel Corporation | INTC |
| Coca-Cola Bottling Co. | COKE |
| Hershey Foods Corporation | HSY |

### Person Name

Excel can label e-mail addresses of people you sent messages to using Microsoft Outlook.

*Note: After sending an e-mail message to a person using Microsoft Outlook, you may have to restart Outlook and Excel to have Excel label the address with a smart tag.*

| ress | Email |
|------|-------|
| Beach St. | nelson@abccorp.com |
| Pine St. | dmorris@xyzcorp.com |
| Westside St. | eross@xyzcorp.com |

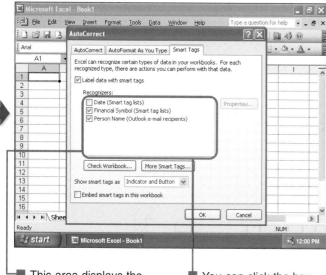

■ This area displays the types of data Excel can label with a smart tag. A check mark (✔) beside a type of data indicates Excel will label the data with a smart tag.

■ You can click the box beside a type of data to add ( ☑ ) or remove ( ☐ ) a check mark.

**5** Click **OK** to confirm your changes.

■ You can now use smart tags in your workbooks.

■ To turn off smart tags for your workbooks, repeat steps **1** to **5** ( ☑ changes to ☐ in step **4**).

*Note: You must close and reopen your open workbooks for the change to take effect in the workbooks. To close a workbook, see page 29. To open a workbook, see page 32.*

# USING SMART TAGS

Excel labels certain types of data, such as financial symbols, with smart tags. You can use a smart tag to perform an action, such as getting a stock price or displaying information about a company.

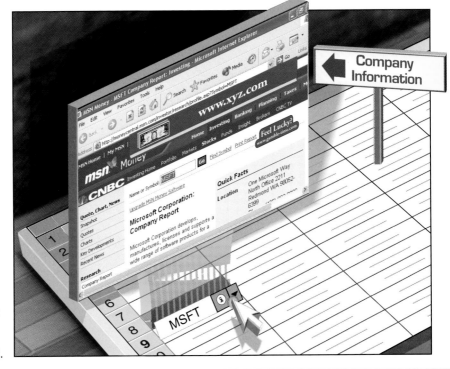

Before you can use smart tags, you must turn on smart tags. For more information, see page 262.

## USING SMART TAGS

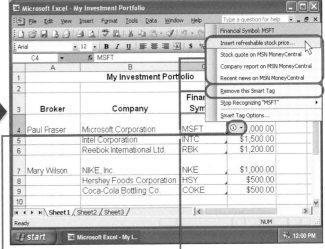

■ A purple triangle appears in the bottom right corner of a cell containing data Excel labels with a smart tag.

**1** To perform an action using a smart tag, click a cell containing a purple triangle.

■ The Smart Tag Actions button appears.

**2** Click the Smart Tag Actions button to display a list of actions you can perform using the smart tag.

**3** Click the action you want to perform.

■ In this example, we insert a refreshable stock price.

■ To remove a smart tag from a cell, click **Remove this Smart Tag**.

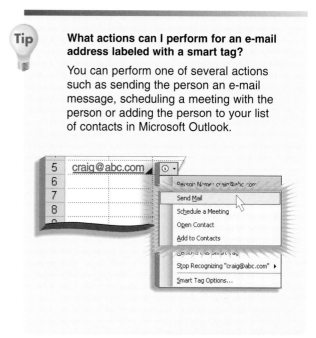

**Tip**

**What actions can I perform for a date labeled with a smart tag?**

You can display your calendar or schedule a meeting in Microsoft Outlook for a date in your worksheet labeled with a smart tag.

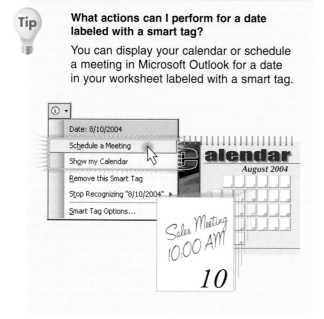

**Tip**

**What actions can I perform for an e-mail address labeled with a smart tag?**

You can perform one of several actions such as sending the person an e-mail message, scheduling a meeting with the person or adding the person to your list of contacts in Microsoft Outlook.

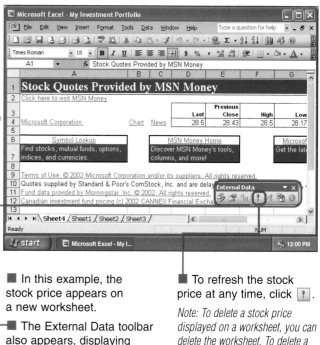

■ The Insert Stock Price dialog box appears.

**4** Click an option to specify where you want the stock price to appear (○ changes to ⦿).

*Note: The stock price may take up a large area of your worksheet.*

**5** Click **OK** to insert the stock price.

■ In this example, the stock price appears on a new worksheet.

■ The External Data toolbar also appears, displaying buttons you can use to work with the stock price.

■ To refresh the stock price at any time, click 🔳.

*Note: To delete a stock price displayed on a worksheet, you can delete the worksheet. To delete a worksheet, see page 173.*

# CREATE A MACRO

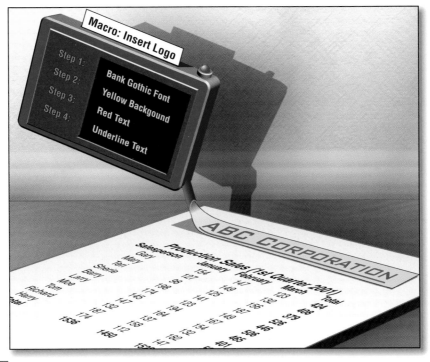

A macro saves you time by combining a series of actions into a single command. Macros are ideal for tasks you frequently perform.

For example, you can create a macro to enter a formula or insert your company logo into your worksheet.

Before creating a macro, you should plan and practice all the actions you want the macro to include.

## CREATE A MACRO

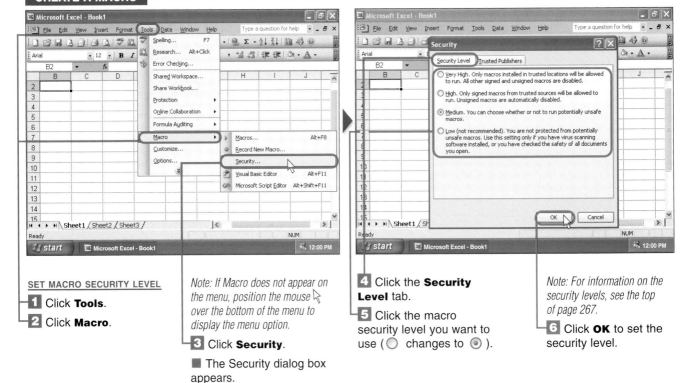

**SET MACRO SECURITY LEVEL**

**1** Click **Tools**.

**2** Click **Macro**.

*Note: If Macro does not appear on the menu, position the mouse over the bottom of the menu to display the menu option.*

**3** Click **Security**.

■ The Security dialog box appears.

**4** Click the **Security Level** tab.

**5** Click the macro security level you want to use (○ changes to ◉).

*Note: For information on the security levels, see the top of page 267.*

**6** Click **OK** to set the security level.

**Tip**

**Why should I set the macro security level?**

Some macros may contain viruses that could damage your computer. Setting the macro security level can help protect your computer from viruses.

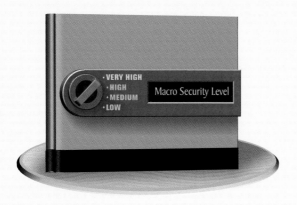

**Very High**

Excel enables only macros from trusted sources and disables all other macros in the workbooks you open.

**High**

Excel enables only macros that are digitally signed in the workbooks you open.

**Medium**

You can disable or enable the macros in the workbooks you open.

**Low**

Excel automatically enables the macros in the workbooks you open.

**RECORD A MACRO**

**1** Click **Tools**.

**2** Click **Macro**.

*Note: If Macro does not appear on the menu, position the mouse over the bottom of the menu to display the menu option.*

**3** Click **Record New Macro**.

■ The Record Macro dialog box appears.

**4** Type a name for the macro.

*Note: A macro name must begin with a letter and cannot contain spaces. A macro name cannot be a cell reference.*

**CONTINUED**

# CREATE A MACRO

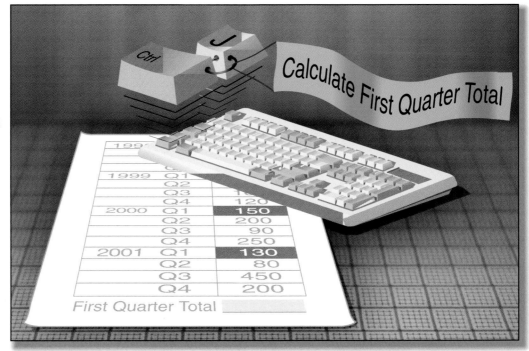

You can assign a keyboard shortcut, such as Ctrl+j, to a macro you create. A keyboard shortcut allows you to quickly run the macro.

**5** To assign a keyboard shortcut to the macro, click this area and then type a lowercase letter you want to use with the `Ctrl` key as the shortcut.

**6** To enter a description for the macro, drag the mouse I over the text in this area until you highlight the text. Then type a description.

**7** Click this area to specify the location where you want to store the macro.

**8** Click the location where you want to store the macro.

*Note: For information on where you can store a macro, see the top of page 269.*

**9** Click **OK** to continue.

## Tip

**Where can I store a macro?**

**Personal Macro Workbook**

If you want to use a macro with all your workbooks, you can store the macro in the Personal Macro Workbook.

**New Workbook**

You can have Excel create a new workbook to store the macro. You will only be able to use the macro when the new workbook is open.

**This Workbook**

You can store the macro in the current workbook. You will only be able to use the macro when this workbook is open.

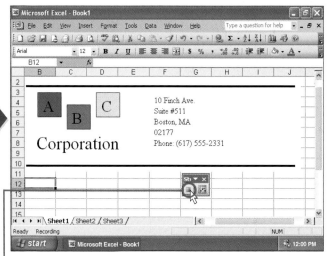

■ The Stop Recording toolbar appears.

**10** Perform the actions you want the macro to include.

**11** Click ▣ when you have completed all the actions you want the macro to include.

■ You can now run the macro. To run a macro, see page 270.

# RUN A MACRO

When you run a macro, Excel automatically performs the actions you recorded.

You should save your workbook before running a macro. After the macro runs, you will not be able to use the Undo feature to reverse the results of the macro or any changes you made before running the macro.

## RUN A MACRO

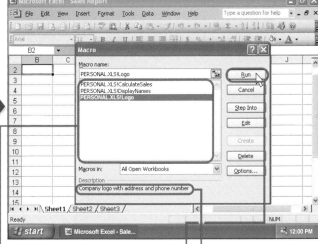

**1** If you want the macro to affect specific cells in your worksheet, select the cells you want to change. To select cells, see page 10.

**2** Click **Tools**.

**3** Click **Macro**.

*Note: If Macro does not appear on the menu, position the mouse over the bottom of the menu to display the menu option.*

**4** Click **Macros**.

■ The Macro dialog box appears.

■ This area displays the available macros. Macros you stored in the Personal Macro Workbook begin with PERSONAL.XLS!.

**5** Click the name of the macro you want to run.

■ This area displays a description of the macro you selected.

**6** Click **Run** to run the macro.

**Tip**

**Why does this dialog box appear when I open a workbook containing a macro?**

This dialog box may appear when you set your macro security level to Medium. To open the workbook, click one of the following options.

■ If the workbook is not from a trusted source, click **Disable Macros** to open the workbook without the macros.

■ If the workbook is from a trusted source, click **Enable Macros** to open the workbook with the macros.

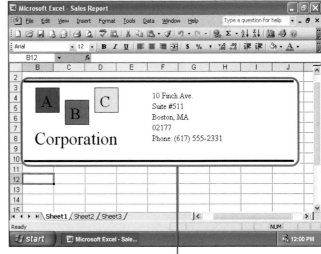

■ The macro performs the actions you recorded.

■ In this example, the macro entered company information into the worksheet.

**RUN A MACRO USING THE KEYBOARD SHORTCUT**

**1** If you want the macro to affect specific cells in your worksheet, select the cells you want to change. To select cells, see page 10.

**2** Press the keyboard shortcut you assigned to the macro.

■ The macro performs the actions you recorded.

## CHAPTER 15

# Using Speech Recognition

*Would you like to use your voice to enter data into a worksheet? Read this chapter to learn how to enter data and select commands using your voice.*

# SET UP SPEECH RECOGNITION

I am using Office Speech Recognition.

Speech recognition allows you to use your voice to enter data into a worksheet and select commands from menus and toolbars. Before you can use speech recognition, you must set up the feature on your computer.

You can set up speech recognition in Microsoft Word, a word processing program included in the Microsoft Office 2003 suite. Once speech recognition is set up, the feature will be available in Excel.

Before setting up speech recognition, make sure your microphone and speakers are connected to your computer.

## SET UP SPEECH RECOGNITION

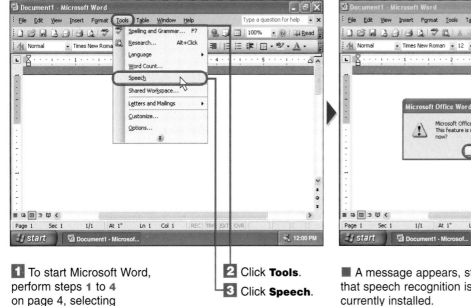

**1** To start Microsoft Word, perform steps **1** to **4** on page 4, selecting **Microsoft Office Word 2003** in step **4**.

**2** Click **Tools**.

**3** Click **Speech**.

■ A message appears, stating that speech recognition is not currently installed.

**4** Click **Yes** to install speech recognition on your computer.

**Tip**

### What are the minimum hardware requirements for using speech recognition?

Speech recognition requires a 400 MHz computer with at least 128 MB of memory to run. You cannot set up speech recognition if your computer does not meet the minimum hardware requirements.

**Tip**

### What type of microphone should I use with speech recognition?

You should use a high quality headset microphone that supports gain adjustment. Gain adjustment allows your computer to automatically make your speech louder. For best results, you should position the microphone approximately one inch from the side of your mouth so that you are not breathing directly into the microphone.

■ When the installation is complete, the Welcome to Office Speech Recognition dialog box appears.

■ This area describes the process of setting up speech recognition on your computer.

**5** To begin setting up speech recognition, click **Next**.

■ The Microphone Wizard appears. The wizard will help you adjust your microphone for use with speech recognition.

■ This area describes the wizard and provides instructions for positioning your microphone.

**6** To begin adjusting your microphone, click **Next**.

**CONTINUED**

# SET UP SPEECH RECOGNITION

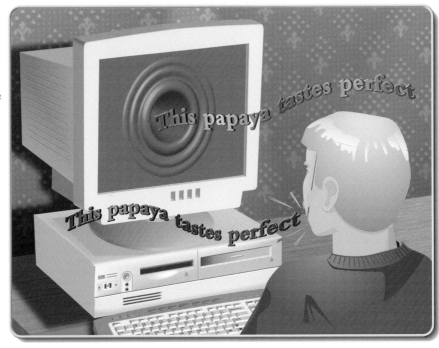

**The Microphone Wizard helps you adjust the volume and position of your microphone for best results with speech recognition.**

Once your microphone is properly set up, you can follow the step-by-step instructions in the Microsoft Speech Recognition Training Wizard to train speech recognition to recognize how you speak.

## SET UP SPEECH RECOGNITION (CONTINUED)

**7** Read the text displayed in this area aloud to adjust the volume of your microphone.

■ As you read the text aloud, the volume meter in this area indicates the volume of your microphone.

**8** Repeat step **7** until a message appears in this area, indicating that the volume level is tuned to your voice.

**9** Click **Next** to continue.

**10** Read this text aloud to test the position of your microphone.

■ After a few moments, your voice will be played back to you. If it sounds like you are blowing into the microphone, adjust your microphone's position and then repeat step **10**.

**Tip**

**Do I have to train speech recognition?**

If you do not train speech recognition, the feature may not work properly. During the training, the Microsoft Speech Recognition Training Wizard gathers information about your voice. The speech recognition feature uses this information to recognize the words you say when entering data or selecting commands.

**Tip**

**How should I speak during the training process?**

You should speak in your everyday tone of voice, pronouncing words clearly and not pausing between words. You should also speak at a consistent speed.

■ If you change the position of your microphone, click **Back** and then repeat steps **7** to **10** to adjust the volume of the microphone in the new position.

**23** When you finish positioning your microphone, click **Finish**.

■ The Voice Training dialog box appears.

■ This area describes the Microsoft Speech Recognition Training Wizard.

**12** To begin training speech recognition to recognize how you speak, click **Next**.

**CONTINUED**

# SET UP SPEECH RECOGNITION

The Microsoft Speech Recognition Training Wizard provides text you can read aloud to train speech recognition.

You should train speech recognition in a quiet area so that background noise does not interfere with the sound of your voice.

## SET UP SPEECH RECOGNITION (CONTINUED)

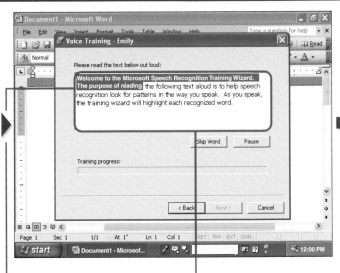

■ This area describes the training process.

**13** To hear a sample of how you should speak during the training, click **Sample**.

**14** Click **Next** to continue.

■ The training wizard will display a series of screens containing text for you to read aloud.

**15** Read the text displayed in this area of each screen.

■ As you read aloud, the training wizard highlights the words it recognizes.

■ If the training wizard does not recognize a word, it stops highlighting the text. If this happens, begin reading again, starting with the first word that is not highlighted.

**Tip**

**I have repeated a word several times, but the wizard still does not recognize the word. What should I do?**

If the wizard cannot recognize a word you say, you can click the **Skip Word** button to move on to the next word.

**Tip**

**Can I perform more training?**

Microsoft Speech Recognition provides additional training sessions you can perform to improve the accuracy of speech recognition.

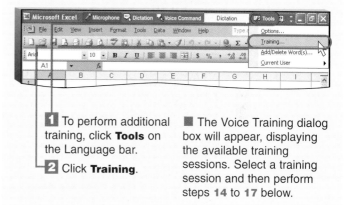

■ To perform additional training, click **Tools** on the Language bar.

**2** Click **Training**.

■ The Voice Training dialog box will appear, displaying the available training sessions. Select a training session and then perform steps **14** to **17** below.

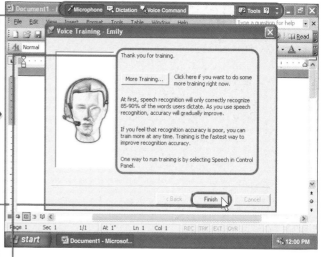

■ To take a break during the training, click **Pause**.

*Note: To resume the training, click Resume.*

■ This area displays the progress of the training.

■ When all the text in this area is highlighted, the training wizard automatically displays the next screen of text.

**16** Repeat step **15** until you have read all the training text.

■ This message appears when the training is complete.

**17** Click **Finish** to close the Voice Training dialog box.

■ This area displays the Language bar, which contains buttons you can use to perform tasks using speech recognition.

■ You can now use speech recognition in Excel.

*Note: A window will appear, displaying a video that introduces you to speech recognition. When the video is finished, click ⊠ to close the window.*

# USING DICTATION MODE

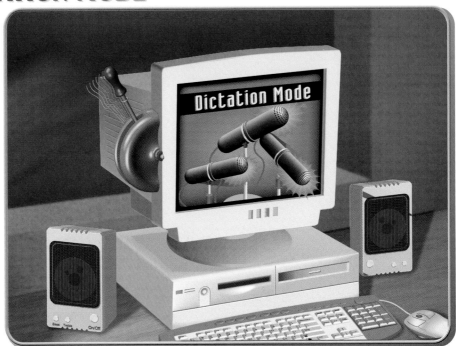

**Once you have set up speech recognition, you can use Dictation mode to enter data into a worksheet using your voice.**

Speech recognition is designed to be used along with your mouse and keyboard. You can use your voice to enter data into a worksheet and then use your mouse and keyboard to edit the data you entered.

## USING DICTATION MODE

**1** If your microphone is turned off, click **Microphone** on the Language bar to turn on the microphone.

*Note: When your microphone is turned on, the Dictation and Voice Command buttons appear on the Language bar.*

**2** Click a cell where you want to enter data using your voice.

**3** Click **Dictation** to turn on Dictation mode.

**4** Speak into your microphone to enter data into the cell.

■ As you speak, a gray bar appears on the screen to indicate that the computer is processing your voice. You can continue to speak while the gray bar is displayed on the screen.

■ You should not use your mouse or keyboard while the gray bar is displayed on the screen.

**What are some of the symbols I can enter using my voice?**

| To enter: | Say: |
|-----------|------|
| = | "Equals" |
| + | "Plus sign" |
| % | "Percent sign" |
| $ | "Dollar sign" |
| > | "Greater than" |
| < | "Less than" |
| ( | "Open parenthesis" |
| ) | "Close parenthesis" |

**How should I speak when using speech recognition?**

You should speak to your computer in your everyday tone of voice, pronouncing words clearly and not pausing between words. You should also speak at a consistent speed. If you speak too quickly or too slowly, the computer may not be able to recognize what you say.

■ As the computer processes your voice, words appear on the screen.

**5** To enter data into another cell using your voice, click the cell.

**6** To enter a symbol, say the name of the symbol.

*Note: For a list of symbols you can enter, see the top of this page.*

**7** To enter a number, say the number you want to enter.

*Note: Numbers less than 20 are entered as words. Numbers greater than 20 are entered as digits.*

**8** When you finish entering data using your voice, click **Microphone** to turn off your microphone.

■ You can now edit the data you entered using your voice as you would edit any data. To edit data, see page 38.

# USING VOICE COMMAND MODE

You can use Voice Command mode to select commands from menus and toolbars using your voice.

You can also use Voice Command mode to select options in dialog boxes.

## USING VOICE COMMAND MODE

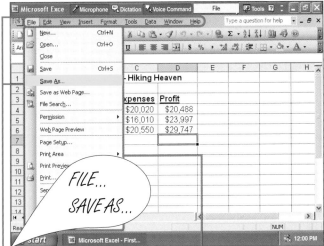

**1** If your microphone is turned off, click **Microphone** on the Language bar to turn on the microphone.

*Note: When your microphone is turned on, the Dictation and Voice Command buttons appear on the Language bar.*

**2** Click **Voice Command** to turn on Voice Command mode.

### SELECT MENU COMMANDS

**1** To select a command from a menu, say the name of the menu.

■ A short version of the menu appears, displaying the most commonly used commands.

*Note: To expand the menu and display all the commands, say "expand."*

**2** To select a command from the menu, say the name of the command.

■ To close a menu without selecting a command, say "escape."

**Tip**

**Can I use Voice Command mode to select an option in a task pane?**

Yes. Task panes display links that allow you to perform common tasks. To select a link in a task pane using your voice, say the full name of the link. For more information on task panes, see page 16.

**Tip**

**Can I use Voice Command mode to perform other tasks?**

In addition to selecting commands, you can use Voice Command mode to change the active cell.

| To: | Say: |
|---|---|
| Move down one cell | "Down" or "Enter" |
| Move up one cell | "Up" |
| Move left one cell | "Left" |
| Move right one cell | "Right" |

**SELECT TOOLBAR COMMANDS**

■ 1 To select a command from a toolbar, say the name of the toolbar button.

■ To determine the name of a toolbar button, position the mouse over the button. After a few seconds, the name of the button appears in a yellow box.

**SELECT DIALOG BOX OPTIONS**

■ A dialog box may appear when you select a menu or toolbar command.

■ 1 To select an option in a dialog box, say the name of the option.

■ If the dialog box contains tabs, you can say the name of a tab to display the tab.

■ 2 When you finish selecting commands using your voice, click **Microphone** to turn off your microphone.

# USING TEXT TO SPEECH

You can have your computer read the data in your worksheet back to you. This can help you confirm that you entered the data correctly.

Before using the text to speech feature, make sure your speakers are connected to your computer.

## USING TEXT TO SPEECH

**1** Select the cells containing the data you want your computer to read back to you. To select cells, see page 10.

**2** Click **Tools**.

**3** Click **Speech**.

*Note: If Speech does not appear on the menu, position the mouse over the bottom of the menu to display the menu option.*

**4** Click **Show Text To Speech Toolbar**.

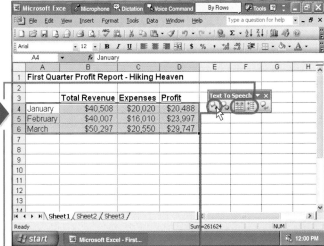

■ The Text To Speech toolbar appears.

**5** Click a button to specify how you want your computer to read data back to you.

Read data by rows

Read data by columns

**6** Click to have your computer read the data in the selected cells back to you.

**How can I have my computer read data back to me as I enter data into cells?**

**1** Perform steps **2** to **4** below to display the Text To Speech toolbar.

**2** Click to have your computer read data back to you as you enter data into cells.

■ You can click again to stop your computer from reading data you enter into cells.

**Tip**

**Will my computer read data in hidden rows or columns?**

No. Your computer will not read data in hidden rows or columns. For information on hiding rows and columns, see page 74.

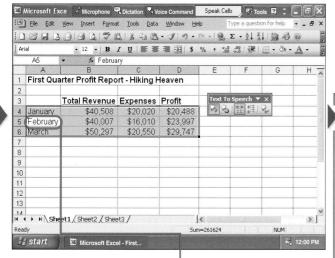

■ Your computer reads the data in the selected cells.

■ The cell your computer is currently reading is highlighted.

■ To stop your computer from reading data back to you, click .

*Note: You can click to once again have your computer read data back to you.*

**7** When your computer finishes reading data back to you, click ✕ to hide the Text To Speech toolbar.

# Excel and the Internet

*Are you wondering how you can use Excel to share data with other people on the Internet? In this chapter, you will learn how to e-mail a worksheet, save a workbook as a Web page and more.*

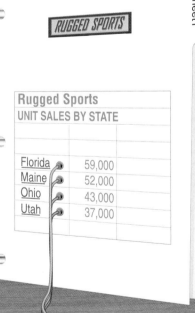

# E-MAIL A WORKSHEET

You can e-mail the worksheet displayed on your screen to exchange data with a friend, family member or colleague.

When you e-mail a worksheet, the worksheet appears in the body of the e-mail message.

Before you can e-mail a worksheet, Microsoft Office Outlook 2003 must be set up on your computer.

## E-MAIL A WORKSHEET

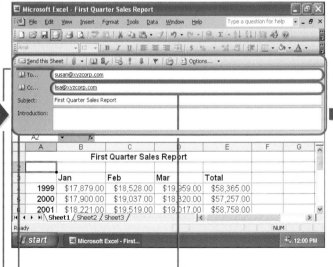

**1** Click 🖃 to e-mail the current worksheet.

*Note: If 🖃 is not displayed, click 🔅 on the Standard toolbar to display the button.*

■ If the workbook contains data on more than one worksheet, a dialog box appears, asking if you want to send the entire workbook or just the current worksheet.

**2** Click this option to send the current worksheet.

**3** Click **OK**.

■ An area appears for you to address the message.

**4** Click this area and type the e-mail address of the person you want to receive the message.

**5** To send a copy of the message to a person who is not directly involved but would be interested in the message, click this area and type the e-mail address.

*Note: To enter more than one e-mail address in step 4 or 5, separate each e-mail address with a semicolon (;).*

**Tip**

**Why would I include an introduction for a worksheet I am e-mailing?**

Including an introduction allows you to provide the recipient of the message with additional information about the worksheet. For example, the recipient may require instructions or an explanation of the content of the worksheet.

**Tip**

**How do I e-mail an entire workbook?**

To e-mail an entire workbook, perform steps **1** to **6** below, selecting **Send the entire workbook as an attachment** in step **2**. Then click **Send** to send the message. When you e-mail an entire workbook, the workbook is sent as an attached file.

**6** Click this area and type a subject for the message.

*Note: If a subject already exists, you can drag the mouse I over the existing subject and then type a new subject.*

**7** To include an introduction for the worksheet you are e-mailing, click this area and type the introduction.

**8** Click **Send this Sheet** to send the message.

*Note: If you are not currently connected to the Internet, a dialog box will appear allowing you to connect.*

# CREATE A HYPERLINK

**You can create a hyperlink to connect data in your workbook to another document on your computer, network, corporate intranet or the Internet.**

Hyperlinks are also known as links.

You can easily identify hyperlinks in your workbook. Hyperlinks appear underlined and in color.

An intranet is a small version of the Internet within a company or organization.

## CREATE A HYPERLINK

**1** Select the cells containing the data you want to make a hyperlink. To select cells, see page 10.

**2** Click ![icon] to create a hyperlink.

*Note: If ![icon] is not displayed, click ![icon] on the Standard toolbar to display the button.*

■ The Insert Hyperlink dialog box appears.

**3** Click **Existing File or Web Page** to link the data to an existing document.

■ This area shows the location of the displayed documents. You can click this area to change the location.

**4** To link the data to a document on your computer or network, click the document in this area.

290

**Tip**

### Can I select a cell that contains a hyperlink?

Yes. Excel allows you to select a cell that contains a hyperlink without displaying the document or Web page connected to the hyperlink. This is useful when you want to change the format of a hyperlink. To select a cell that contains a hyperlink, position the mouse 🖑 over the cell and then hold down the left mouse button until the mouse 🖑 changes to ⊕.

**Tip**

### Can Excel automatically create a hyperlink for me?

When you type a Web page address in an Excel worksheet, Excel will automatically change the address to a hyperlink for you.

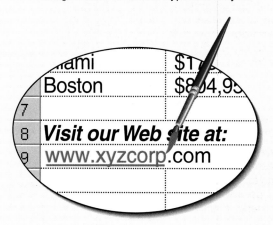

*Visit our Web site at:*
www.xyzcorp.com

---

■ To link the data to a page on the Web, click this area and then type the address of the Web page (example: www.maran.com).

**5** Click **OK** to create the hyperlink.

■ Excel creates the hyperlink. Hyperlinks appear underlined and in color.

■ When you position the mouse 🖑 over a hyperlink, a yellow box appears, indicating where the hyperlink will take you.

■ You can click the hyperlink to display the document or Web page connected to the hyperlink.

*Note: If the hyperlink connects to a Web page, your Web browser will open and display the page.*

# PREVIEW A WORKBOOK AS A WEB PAGE

You can preview how your workbook will look as a Web page. This allows you to see how the workbook will appear on the Internet or your company's intranet.

An intranet is a small version of the Internet within a company or organization.

## PREVIEW A WORKBOOK AS A WEB PAGE

**1** Open the workbook you want to preview as a Web page. To open a workbook, see page 32.

**2** Click **File**.

**3** Click **Web Page Preview** to preview your workbook as a Web page.

**Tip**

### Will my Web page look the same when displayed in different Web browsers?

No. Different Web browsers may display your Web page differently. There are many Web browsers used on the Web.

**Tip**

### Can I make changes to a workbook I am previewing as a Web page?

You cannot make changes to a workbook displayed in a Web browser window. If you want to change the way the data appears on the Web page, you must make the changes to the workbook in the Microsoft Excel window and then repeat steps **2** and **3** below to preview the changes in the Web browser window.

■ Your Web browser window opens, displaying your workbook as a Web page.

**4** To maximize the Web browser window to fill your screen, click 🔲 .

■ The gridlines that separate each cell do not appear in the Web browser window.

■ If your workbook contains data on more than one worksheet, this area displays a tab for each worksheet.

**5** To display the contents of a different worksheet, click a tab.

**6** When you finish previewing your workbook as a Web page, click ❌ to close the Web browser window.

# SAVE A WORKBOOK AS A WEB PAGE

You can save a workbook as a Web page. This allows you to place the workbook on the Internet or your company's intranet.

An intranet is a small version of the Internet within a company or organization.

## SAVE A WORKBOOK AS A WEB PAGE

**1** Open the workbook you want to save as a Web page. To open a workbook, see page 32.

**2** Click **File**.

**3** Click **Save as Web Page**.

■ The Save As dialog box appears.

**4** Type a file name for the Web page.

■ This area shows the location where Excel will store the Web page. You can click this area to change the location.

■ This area allows you to access commonly used locations. You can click a location to save the Web page in the location.

*Note: For information on the commonly used locations, see the top of page 23.*

**What is the difference between the file name and the title of a Web page?**

The file name is the name you use to store the Web page on your computer. The title is the text that will appear at the top of the Web browser window when a person views your Web page.

**How do I make my Web page available for other people to view?**

After you save your workbook as a Web page, you can transfer the page to a computer that stores Web pages, called a Web server. Once the Web page is stored on a Web server, the page will be available for other people to view. For information on transferring a Web page to a Web server, contact your network administrator or Internet service provider.

**5** Click **Change Title** to specify a title for the Web page.

■ The Set Page Title dialog box appears.

**6** Type a title for the Web page.

**7** Click **OK** to confirm the title.

■ This area displays the title you specified for the Web page.

**8** Click an option to specify whether you want to save the entire workbook or just the current worksheet as a Web page (○ changes to ⦿).

**9** Click **Save** to save the Web page.

# INDEX

# INDEX

# INDEX

# INDEX

## illustrated PIANO

**MARAN ILLUSTRATED™ Piano** is an information-packed resource for people who want to learn to play the piano, as well as current musicians looking to hone their skills. Combining full-color photographs and easy-to-follow instructions, this guide covers everything from the basics of piano playing to more advanced techniques. Not only does MARAN ILLUSTRATED™ Piano show you how to read music, play scales and chords and improvise while playing with other musicians, it also provides you with helpful information for purchasing and caring for your piano.

ISBN: 1-59200-864-X

Price: $24.99 US;   $33.95 CDN

Page count: 304

## illustrated DOG TRAINING

**MARAN ILLUSTRATED™ Dog Training** is an excellent guide for both current dog owners and people considering making a dog part of their family. Using clear, step-by-step instructions accompanied by over 400 full-color photographs, MARAN ILLUSTRATED™ Dog Training is perfect for any visual learner who prefers seeing what to do rather than reading lengthy explanations.

Beginning with insights into popular dog breeds and puppy development, this book emphasizes positive training methods to guide you through socializing, housetraining and teaching your dog many commands. You will also learn how to work with problem behaviors, such as destructive chewing.

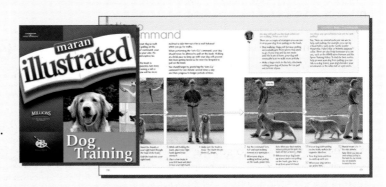

ISBN: 1-59200-858-5

Price: $19.99 US;   $26.95 CDN

Page count: 256

**MARAN ILLUSTRATED™ Knitting & Crocheting** contains a wealth of information about these two increasingly popular crafts. Whether you are just starting out or you are an experienced knitter or crocheter interested in picking up new tips and techniques, this information-packed resource will take you from the basics, such as how to hold the knitting needles or crochet hook, to more advanced skills, such as how to add decorative touches to your projects. The easy-to-follow information is communicated through clear, step-by-step instructions and accompanied by over 600 full-color photographs—perfect for any visual learner.

ISBN: 1-59200-862-3
Price: $24.99 US; $33.95 CDN
Page count: 304

**MARAN ILLUSTRATED™ Yoga** provides a wealth of simplified, easy-to-follow information about the increasingly popular practice of Yoga. This easy-to-use guide is a must for visual learners who prefer to see and do without having to read lengthy explanations.

Using clear, step-by-step instructions accompanied by over 500 full-color photographs, this book includes all the information you need to get started with yoga or to enhance your technique if you have already made yoga a part of your life. MARAN ILLUSTRATED™ Yoga shows you how to safely and effectively perform a variety of yoga poses at various skill levels, how to breathe more efficiently and much more.

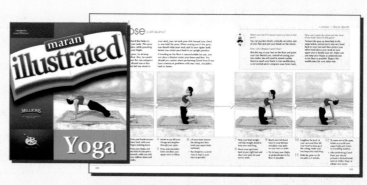

ISBN: 1-59200-868-2
Price: $24.99 US; $33.95 CDN
Page count: 320

## maran illustrated WEIGHT TRAINING

**MARAN ILLUSTRATED™ Weight Training** is an information-packed guide that covers all the basics of weight training, as well as more advanced techniques and exercises.

MARAN ILLUSTRATED™ Weight Training contains more than 500 full-color photographs of exercises for every major muscle group, along with clear, step-by-step instructions for performing the exercises. Useful tips provide additional information and advice to help enhance your weight training experience.

MARAN ILLUSTRATED™ Weight Training provides all the information you need to start weight training or to refresh your technique if you have been weight training for some time.

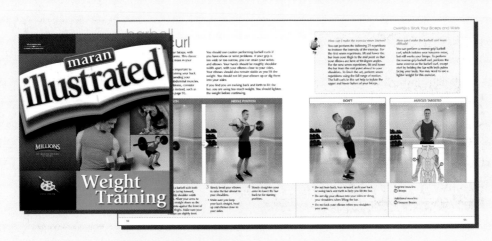

ISBN: 1-59200-866-6

Price: $24.99 US;  $33.95 CDN

Page count: 320

GUITAR

**MARAN ILLUSTRATED**™ **Guitar** is an excellent resource for people who want to learn to play the guitar, as well as for current musicians who want to fine tune their technique. This full-color guide includes over 500 photographs, accompanied by step-by-step instructions that teach you the basics of playing the guitar and reading music, as well as advanced guitar techniques. You will also learn what to look for when purchasing a guitar or accessories, how to maintain and repair your guitar, and much more.

Whether you want to learn to strum your favorite tunes or play professionally, MARAN ILLUSTRATED™ Guitar provides all the information you need to become a proficient guitarist.

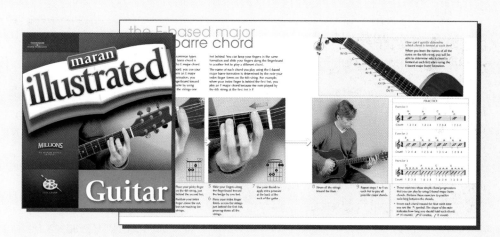

ISBN: 1-59200-860-7
Price: $24.99 US; $33.95 CDN
Page count: 320

Did you like this book? MARAN ILLUSTRATED™ offers books on the most popular computer topics, using the same easy-to-use format of this book. We always say that if you like one of our books, you'll love the rest of our books too!

Here's a list of some of our best-selling computer titles:

## Guided Tour Series - 240 pages, Full Color

**MARAN ILLUSTRATED's Guided Tour series features a friendly disk character that walks you through each task step by step. The full-color screen shots are larger than in any of our other series and are accompanied by clear, concise instructions.**

| | ISBN | Price |
|---|---|---|
| MARAN ILLUSTRATED™ Computers Guided Tour | 1-59200-880-1 | $24.99 US/$33.95 CDN |
| MARAN ILLUSTRATED™ Windows XP Guided Tour | 1-59200-886-0 | $24.99 US/$33.95 CDN |

## MARAN ILLUSTRATED™ Series - 320 pages, Full Color

**This series covers 30% more content than our Guided Tour series. Learn new software fast using our step-by-step approach and easy-to-understand text. Learning programs has never been this easy!**

| | ISBN | Price |
|---|---|---|
| MARAN ILLUSTRATED™ Windows XP | 1-59200-870-4 | $24.99 US/$33.95 CDN |
| MARAN ILLUSTRATED™ Office 2003 | 1-59200-890-9 | $29.99 US/$40.95 CDN |
| MARAN ILLUSTRATED™ Excel 2003 | 1-59200-876-3 | $24.99 US/$33.95 CDN |
| MARAN ILLUSTRATED™ Access 2003 | 1-59200-872-0 | $24.99 US/$33.95 CDN |

## 101 Hot Tips Series - 240 pages, Full Color

**Progress beyond the basics with MARAN ILLUSTRATED's 101 Hot Tips series. This series features 101 of the coolest shortcuts, tricks and tips that will help you work faster and easier.**

| | ISBN | Price |
|---|---|---|
| MARAN ILLUSTRATED™ Windows XP 101 Hot Tips | 1-59200-882-8 | $19.99 US/$26.95 CDN |